SAM AND THE 100th BOMB GROUP

SAM HURRY and MALCOLM FINNIS

Copyright Sam Hurry and Malcolm Finnis 2009
Copyright cover painting 'Home At Last' Joe Crowfoot 2009

Published by:
100th Bomb Group Memorial Museum,
Common Road,
Dickleburgh.
Diss,
Norfolk IP21 4PH

www.100bgmus.org.uk

ISBN 0-9515159-1-8
978-0-9515159-1-4

Illustrations: the credits are shown in brackets

Other books by Malcolm Finnis:
The Six Eighty First Comes Back
Twilight Of The Pistons – Air Ferry A Manston Airline
Take-off To Touchdown – The Invicta Airlines Story

DEDICATION

This story is dedicated to the Hurry and Taylor families, and all the Americans who served at Thorpe Abbotts, especially the ones who gave their lives in the cause of victory.

APPRECIATION

I would like to thank all those who contributed to, or supported, the production of this book, especially Malcolm Finnis for his continual encouragement and assembly of the written word, to David and Mrs Hurry, Raymond Hubbard, Peggy Taylor, the 100th Bomb Group Memorial Museum for helping out with photographs and indeed my fellow trustees of the museum.

Particular thanks to artist Joe Crowfoot for permission to use detail from an original painting on the front cover, Joe can be contacted through www.joecrowfootartist@yahoo.co.uk

I thank you all, I hope you enjoy reading this book as I have enjoyed writing it.

Sam Hurry

INTRODUCTION

Much has been written about the 100th Bomb Group of the American Eighth Army Air Force that operated from Thorpe Abbotts in Norfolk during the Second World War. Aircrew have recounted their aerial exploits, engineers and other service personnel have added their contributions while historians have attempted to portray an overall critique of those eventful days.

However, until now one narrative has been missing; one told from the viewpoint of the local civilians and, more especially, as seen through the eyes of two young boys who spent more time on one of the sixty eight wartime airfields used by the Eighth than could be imagined.

Many of the stories have a humorous side but this was not always so. Grim events occurred on military airfields and the boys were vividly aware of these. It is important to stress that the events they witnessed were carried out by men attempting to demonstrate that daylight precision bombing was not only possible but a vital contribution to winning the war. Many battle-scarred veterans of the first three years of war considered the evidence proved that the concept was doomed to failure.

It is not the intention to re-tell the story of the 'Bloody Hundredth,' as the 100th Bomb Group was called, and the Eighth Air Force within these pages but, so that the reader may be aware of the background as to why the Americans came to Thorpe Abbotts, and why they operated by day; it is necessary to go back briefly to chart some earlier events.

As the war clouds gathered over Europe during the 1930s a number of expansion schemes were implemented by the R.A.F. New types of aircraft were put into production and new airfields were planned and constructed.

When the Bristol Blenheim bomber entered service in 1937 it could easily outpace the fighters of the time, reinforcing the theories that: 'The bomber will always get through' and that daylight bombing was a feasible proposition. Hostilities broke out in September 1939 and operations by Bomber Command Wellingtons and Hampdens in the early months of the war suffered some heavy losses, as did the gallant Battles and Blenheims of the Advanced Air Striking Force during the invasion of France in May 1940. The valiant daytime operations of Bomber Command against the occupied Channel Ports during the Battle of Britain also suffered a high casualty rate.

As a result, although there were exceptions, Bomber Command turned increasingly to night operations to gain some protection from the cloak of darkness, as did the Luftwaffe following its defeat in the Battle of Britain. By April 1942, when Sir Arthur Harris became Commander in Chief of Bomber Command, the force had new four-engined bombers with new equipment and was building up to the colossal force that it would be by the end of the war in Europe in May 1945.

To provide facilities for this growth in R.A.F. strength, and to meet the American requirements, hundreds of new airfields were constructed across Great Britain during the years 1938-1944 in the largest civil engineering construction project ever known. In Norfolk, as in other counties, the pre-war R.A.F. stations were rapidly outnumbered by new ones.

Across the Atlantic, a controversy over bombing had been raging for many years with ardent supporters for the theory that strategic bombardment would be a conclusive feature in future conflicts. New equipment, such as the Boeing B-17 Flying Fortress and the highly secret Norden bombsight convinced many generals in the U.S.A.A.F. that the theory of daylight precision bombing could be proven if the opportunity arose.

While America was still at peace, liaison between the R.A.F. and the U.S.A.A.F. was close with the R.A.F. benefitting from lease-lend equipment and the U.S.A.A.F. studying R.A.F. operational procedures. General Ira C. Eaker was deeply involved in discussions with the British regarding American involvement in the event of the U.S.A. entering the war.

The Japanese attack on the U.S. naval installations at Pearl Harbour on 7 December 1941 precipitated America into the conflict that now widened into a world war. In April 1942 a Douglas DC-3 made the dangerous journey from Lisbon to Britain carrying seven U.S.A.A.F. officers, including General Eaker and Captain Beirne Lay Jr., to set up the American Eighth Air Force. The Eighth would operate four-engined bombers and long range escort fighters from airfields across Britain.

After some months of preparation the first bombing raid by the U.S.A.A.F. was carried out on 17 August 1942 by the 97th Bomb Group operating from Grafton Underwood in Northamptonshire. The build up of the new force was relatively slow as U.S. operational requirements were massive and covered vast areas of the world's surface.

'THE MIGHTY EIGHTH' by Roger A. Freeman

'From November 1942 to May 1943 the American daylight bomber offensive from England was carried out largely by four B-17 Groups.'

The Casablanca Conference of January 1943 laid down the policy for the conduct of the war and led to the frightening reality of the Axis Powers in Europe being subjected to 'Round the clock bombing' with R.A.F. Bomber Command operating primarily by night and the Eighth's aircraft flying by day on their precision bombing missions.

The organisational structure of the Eighth Air Force evolved into three Air Divisions with the 1st Division Headquarters in Huntingdonshire, the 2nd Division H.Q. at Ketteringham Hall, Norfolk and the 3rd Division H.Q. at Elveden Hall in Suffolk.

Each Division was made up of Combat Wings with each Wing usually comprising three Bomb Groups. Thus the 100th Bomb Group from Thorpe Abbotts flew with the 95th Bomb Group from Horham and the 390th Bomb Group from Framlingham as the 13th Combat Wing of the 3rd Air Division of the 8th Air Force.

The R.A.F. Bomber Command practice was for two squadrons to be based at one airfield while the American Groups, that each consisted of four squadrons, had an airfield each.

'THE MIGHTY EIGHTH' by Roger A. Freeman

The 100th Bomb Group was at Thorpe Abbotts from 9 June 1943 to 11 December 1945. The 100th was made up of four Squadrons, the 349th, 350th, 351st and 418th.

They flew 306 missions, with 177 aircraft missing in action and 52 other operational losses.

Two major awards were given to the Group, Distinguished Unit Citations for the missions to Regensburg in August 1943 and Berlin in March 1944.

The 100th had an unfortunate claim to fame in that it suffered spectacular heavy losses at intervals throughout the period of combat.

Life in pre-war East Anglia was largely centred on farming and although the new airfields inevitably consumed large areas of prime agricultural land they were constructed with great care to conserve this as much as possible. The construction of an airfield involved the use of prodigious amounts of material while the completed stations were models of engineering expertise, considering the shortage of labour and the use of equipment that was vastly different from construction machinery in use today.

'AIRFIELDS OF THE EIGHTH - THEN AND NOW'

Thorpe Abbotts was laid down as a satellite to Horham in 1942, John Laing & Sons Ltd. did the work, excavating 330,000 cubic yards of soil and putting down 149,000 cubic yards of concrete plus the tarmac area totalling 35,000 yards super. The airfield was brought to Class A Standard on completion with three interconnecting runways encircled by a 3 1/2 mile perimeter track. There were fifty aircraft hardstandings and two T2 hangars in addition to the technical, administrative and domestic sites.

The 100th Bomb Group in formation. (100th BGMM)

SAM'S STORY – IN THE BEGINNING

Pre-Airfield   Pulham Air Station   Prisoners of War
Airfield Construction   Arrival of Americans
Airfield Gates.

The memories recounted for this story are as vivid now as the days on which they happened, notwithstanding that I was eight years old when the airfield construction started and just over nine when the Americans arrived. By the time of my twelfth birthday they had gone and Thorpe Abbotts was already in disrepair and the remorseless contraction of what had been a first line airfield was already well underway.

For me the fascination for the place started early on in my life, I knew every tree and which part of the pond had the biggest fish. There used to be a line of oaks along where part of the airfield would later be constructed and I recall days as a family picking acorns for the local farmer's pigs. We were paid 3d per bushel by the farmer for gathering the acorns.

On an evening in 1942 I lay in bed, fighting off sleep, to listen to the muffled voice of my father downstairs giving news that there was to be an airfield built a mile or so from the village. Dad said: 'They have pulled Grove Cottage down,' and this was the first clue. Grove Cottage was a small home that would have been sited just off the end of one of the two shorter runways, the one angled Southwest/Northeast.

This conversation marked the beginning of an association between me and the airfield which would last long after the war had ended. It heralded a time in my life which would see me unofficially adopted by the American servicemen who welcomed me, sharing a variety of experiences and insights broader than the small village school could provide.

In early 1942, before construction started, the most notable feature of the landscape to the east of the town of Diss was the R.A.F. Station and airship hangar at Pulham St. Mary. This large structure overlooked the land to the south of the station that included the villages of Dickleburgh, Thorpe Abbotts and Billingford.

Pulham St. Mary was the site of Number 53 Maintenance Unit from W.W.I. days. Although an R.A.F. organisation, it was staffed mainly by civilians. A civilian chief executive officer was in charge, backed up by the station commander, (R.A.F.).

The station had several roles during the war. The main purpose of the Maintenance Unit was to service ammunition, shells and bombs. Out of date or damaged ordnance was dismantled and either cleaned and refilled or scrapped. Much of this work was carried out by women and there were stringent inspection routines. Any residue from these processes was burned and they had quite big fires that resulted in a continual pall of black smoke hanging above the site. We never went near where they worked on the explosives. An Air Force bus used to come through the village each morning at seven forty five to pick up the men who worked there and return them in the evenings at five o'clock. The women workers tended to live in Rushall or Pulham and cycle to the Air Station.

Pulham had a Signals Section and there was also a Radio Listening Post on the site. A Sergeant Bush who worked on this lodged with my aunt next door.

Another use was that a Prisoner Of War Camp was located in the vicinity of the Pulham Air Station. The P.O.W.s, mostly German prisoners with some Italians, wore brown tunics and trousers, and later Dad made us wear a tunic to school, complete with the coloured patch on the back that identified the wearer as a P.O.W.

The prisoners made model ships and placed them in bottles. The model was complete with a battery underneath the stand and a bulb to light the background and illuminate the ship. This was operated by a switch on the mount and the switches came off the B-17 dump.

After the Americans came, Pulham would add one more feature on the site, the most exciting of all to us boys.

Irish labourers moved into the area almost overnight and the airfield began to take shape in an amazingly short time. I remember there was a lorry a minute coming along Common Road, Dickleburgh.

Suddenly lots of new people arrived and my familiar countryside began to change, with builders and labourers billeted in the local homes. The narrow lanes and cart tracks accommodated lorries and trucks of all descriptions.

When laid, the western end of the main runway cut across the narrow pre-war lane leading from Common Road, Dickleburgh to Billingford and the road was officially closed off for the duration of the war. This caused some inconvenience to the locals although, as will be shown, not everyone followed this order.

While the airfield was being constructed there was the sound of explosions each day that we could hear at school. Many trees had to be removed and they used to dynamite the roots and blow them out. Each tree that remained after this work had a number painted on the trunk and these were protected against damage or removal. There were whole strips of woodland with all the trees bearing a white number.

From April 1943, when the first Americans arrived into the parish of Thorpe Abbotts, my school attendance became erratic and for some periods of time non-existent. Most days during term time, and every day during the holidays, me and Billy Taylor, my friend, would be somewhere near the airfield, more often than not we would be on it working with some of the Americans. My home was a bike ride away from the airfield and Billy's home was next to a dispersal and fuel loading position. A home close to the airfield was just the base two inquisitive boys needed.

I can remember them coming quite clearly, Billy and I were near the Control Tower. There were a few Americans there, a skeleton staff getting the place ready. Suddenly the sky was full with great airplanes, we had never seen planes as big as this before, with four engines. We stood and watched the huge bombers circle before landing; it was some time before we dared leave the spectacle and go home.

We must have looked like strays to the Americans, we were two forlorn boys looking half starved and dressed scruffily in torn clothing. They asked us if we had eaten that day and we said no. We were lifted into the mess wagon and taken to the mess hall near the Red Cross building. Was I scared, I had never seen so many Americans in one place or so much food before. We waited in line with mess can, plate and eating irons. When our turn came, meat loaf, potatoes, peas, carrots and gravy were put on the plate. Then, to my horror, onto the same plate came peaches and cream. I was astounded at being served all this on the same plate but I soon overcame the shock, the food seemed as if it liked mixing together, it tasted lovely and we travelled many times to the mess hall.

There were three gates to Station 139 as the airfield was called. These airfield gates were placed to control road access and were manned by Military Police sentries. There was one on the corner of Common Road near the Taylors' house, another on the Thorpe Abbotts Road, leading up to the Fuel Store, and the third on the Billingford Road just off the A143 to Great Yarmouth. At no time can I remember being stopped at the gate or refused entry, the guards gave us sweets and chocolate and we went through without any hassle.

Other than the roads, there was nothing in the way of security fencing round the airfield, the boundaries were denoted by hedgerows, trees, dykes and other natural obstructions.

Dickleburgh Rectory Road (The Raymond Hubbard Collection)

Dickleburgh 'Kings Head' (The Raymond Hubbard Collection)

THE FAMILIES
Hurry family   Taylor family   Laundry
Smoking   Draper Family

I was born on 26 February 1934, the third of four boys. Albert was four years my senior, Derek two years older, and Warwick three years younger than myself. Albert was interested in engineering and on starting work went to a local mill, working on heavy oil engines.

My mother, Eleanor, had worked on airships at Pulham Air Station; she had green fingers and was a genius at gardening. She was later asked to look after the Pulham garden with a group of other women.

Ernest Hurry, circa 1916 (Sam Hurry)

My father, Ernest, invariably called Jack, lost his job in a bakery during the National Strike and then went to Pulham Air Station. He worked for the Air Ministry at Pulham as an Aeronautical Inspection Officer, checking the servicing and disposal of the ordnance and was sometimes picked up for work by transport and also brought home.

He was later placed in charge of Prisoners of War at Pulham St. Mary and would occasionally bring a P.O.W. home to tea; I suppose these were the trusted ones. Of the boys, I was the only one interested in these visitors. Father also brought several of the model ships in bottles home and gave them to our relatives. In those days money was short and Dad would sit half the night with mother repairing shoes from car tyres. Later on, when the Luftwaffe bombed the airship hangar at Pulham in daylight, my father was hurt by shrapnel. With four boys, the house was not large enough for a lively family and we moved within Dickleburgh several times, including Common Road.

My great friend was Billy Taylor, some two to three years older than myself, who lived in Common Road. Raymond Hubbard, another friend, lived one mile out from the short runway, at the Dickleburgh end, and

The Hurry Family l-r Sam, Albert, 2 neighbours, Eleanor holding Warwick, Derek
(Sam Hurry)

sometimes went to Thorpe Abbotts with Billy and myself.

George Taylor and his wife, also named Eleanor, had three children, Ginny the eldest, was later conscripted as a nurse in London. Next came George who was directed onto the land and worked for Farmer Draper, while Billy, the youngest, was still at school.

The Americans had a sense of fun and very often used it at the expense of the locals. Some of the aircraft hardstandings were sited near to where civilians cycled by and sometimes the groundcrews would wait until someone was passing by and then run the engines of an aircraft up to full power to see if the draught created was strong enough to unseat the cyclist. Billy's mother was never the victim of such pranks, and not even the might of the American Eighth Air Force could

At one time this was the Hurry Home, Common Road, circa 1950
(Sam Hurry)

stop her from cycling across the airfield to a whist drive in a village on the far side. Mrs. Taylor was a keen whist player and most weeks during the war she would get out her bicycle and go over the airfield to these get-togethers. Quite a normal thing to do until it was noticed that the route she took was directly across the main runway, on the line of the old pre-war lane.

Mrs. Taylor had no fear of aeroplanes, they would be taking off while she happily rode her bicycle behind or in front of them; she was often seen riding her cycle on the perimeter track with an aircraft behind her. I remember when the Provost Marshall, chief of military police, intercepted Billy's mother on her High Emma during one of the weekly crossings of the runway; he was left in no doubt as to who was there first.

Billy's mother always cooked tapioca and I often wondered where the raw material came from. The milk for the puddings was brought home by George, Billy's brother, who was a cowman on Draper's Farm.

The Americans' arrival began an upturn in the local economy and our mothers were quick to realise that they could help the airmen by doing their laundry. My mother and aunt set up a laundry in my home. They had about 50-60 customers and it took two days for the laundry to be ready; I did the fetching and delivering walking from my home to the airfield and round the billets.

Wash day was quite a fun day, we were often kept at home, both in Billy's house and mine, to help out with the washing. Sometimes it was a same day service if we could get it dry. Military issue shirts were considered difficult to launder and I remember that the charge for one was sixpence. On the days that the laundry was done the whole house would be full of steam, and on wet days clothes hung on makeshift lines and almost any available pieces of furniture, which created an obstacle course throughout the house.

My mother did some washing for the aircrews and, given the scale of losses, it was inevitable that occasionally some went uncollected. Mother was very saddened by this and all we could do was take the uncollected items back to the crew's dispersal.

The washing at the Taylors' was done in an annexe to the house. One part housed the copper, heated by a fire underneath, while in another part was a hand operated washing machine. After leaving the copper the clothes were placed inside the machine and agitated by means of sliding handles at the top which caused paddles to beat against the washing. Once production was started, Mrs Taylor was loath to leave the copper and operating the washing machine fell on me, while Billy was getting ready, or to Billy or Mr. Taylor before he left for work.

At Billy's home the drying of clothes presented few problems; being close to a dispersal point it only needed a word to the groundcrew to test the engines of any plane that they happened to be working on and the draught that they caused would be enough to dry a whole line of washing in about ten minutes.

When the laundry was completed it was delivered back to the airfield and new laundry collected. Often the laundry bag contained tins of cheese, butter, ham or fruit as a gift from the Americans; very welcome, indeed all hush, hush.

The close proximity of Billy's house and the regular visits with the laundry led to a growing friendship between me, Billy and the airmen working at the dispersal.

Mrs Taylor did the laundry for Captain Bill Carleton, the 351st Squadron Engineering Officer, and his staff. As their office bounded on to the Taylors' house, a short cut through their garden proved easy access for them when delivering or collecting laundry.

Mr. Taylor had a handcart that Billy and I sometimes used for hauling great piles of laundry. For most of the time we tied the laundry to Billy's mother's bike which was a High Emma, and pushed that on our delivery rounds. Although the details are now sketchy, at some point the Taylors' handcart was stolen. However Mr. Taylor, in his official capacity as a Special Constable, tracked down the miscreant and, so the story goes, handcuffed him to a tree.

Within a few months of the Americans coming; I was all of nine at the time, Billy and I were ardent smokers. Billy liked the tobacco Prince Albert, a 'roll your own' brand, while I liked Chesterfield and Merit. Billy already smoked Woodbines and was always coughing heavily.

I can remember smoking Chesterfield purely as I liked the name. Billy and I would take American cigarettes to school and hand them over to our friends or exchange them for some item. At home, Mother smoked, my aunt smoked, mother's friend smoked, and father smoked all the American brands, Camel, Lucky Strike and Merit.

Billy's father smoked Woodbines and bought them in packs of five cigs from the merry Widow who ran a shop in the village from her kitchen. I do not recall ever seeing her dressed as she always had a dressing gown on, no matter what time of day. Similarly, I cannot remember Billy's father running out of cigarettes, he was a chain smoker, lighting one on average every ten minutes. Billy's brother George also smoked Woodbines so we were raised in smoky conditions.

The Taylors' had two dogs and, while both of these sometimes accompanied us on our travels, one of them, an excellent rabbiter, was invariably with us. He would wait outside any building we went into, such as the Control Tower or the Mess Hall, until we finally reappeared. At other times he could be recalled by a whistle from what seemed miles away.

Billy Draper was the local farmer most involved with the airfield site. His father ran the bakery in the village and later on Billy's brother took over the bakery. Billy had owned Chapel Farm then took over Lodge Farm, a tenant farm at Dickleburgh.

Lodge Farm was situated between the perimeter track and Common Road, with the buildings halfway between the Control Tower and Billy Taylor's house. The survivors of the pre-war line of oak trees were parallel with the perimeter track and between the track and the farm. Some of the higher ups spent time at Billy Draper's house at Lodge Farm, jeeps were often calling there. It may have been connected with the store but Billy had Allis Chalmers farm equipment at the end of the war! It was probably all legal.

Billy Taylor and I had to fetch eggs from Billy Draper's chicken farm at Carlton Grove and it was not always easy as he kept several cockerels and they often attacked us. Hens ran all over the place there but mostly laid their eggs in the barn or a hut, I'm sure we used to leave a chalk mark to record how many we took, but the main problem was not to break any. We collected the eggs in a metal bucket with straw in. The eggs were taken to various dispersal points by arrangement and as you may guess the Americans used a lot of fresh eggs in the tents beside the dispersal points. A meal of ham and eggs was the favourite.

After we had delivered the eggs some illicit trading went on in exchange for them. There was always food being exchanged as well as cigarettes, tins of sugar and tins of cheese, we were never told all the details but it did happen.

SCHOOL PART 1
'Uphill, Downhill' - Dickleburgh School through the eyes of Sam Hurry 1939-1949

The years of being in the infant class at Dickleburgh School hold hardly any memories for me, although I recall the class was situated nearest the playing field.

It was not until I made my way up the stone steps that 'life' started to change and a new world opened up. Bearing in mind that school was our near home for ten years as in those days we did not move schools. There were no 'school dinners', no 'running water' and the 'toilets' were notoriously overrun with flies in summer and snow bound in winter. However there were some 'happy days' and indeed some not so happy days. The recollections are not in any chronological sequence.

During the war there were ninety eight children and six teachers of which two were temporary and some part time. The Head Mistress was Miss Doris Register, a woman I had a love-hate relationship with. Sadly, she was despised by all and her rule was that of a 'Victorian squire.' She taught, caned and drove us into near despair. Miss Register lodged at Dickleburgh during the week and returned to Norwich on Fridays. She

Dickleburgh All Saints Church and School (Raymond Hubbard Collection)

Doris Register's class, Sam second from right front row. Doris Register at left back row (Sam Hurry)

drove an old Ford Popular car that we prayed would break down as she was leaving Norwich; in winter if the weather was bad, she used the bus. From time to time us boys were required to polish the car. Miss Register was a disciplinarian as I never want to see again; however with hindsight, she was a good teacher and I often wondered why she never married.

Miss Orriss taught the infants and was quite the opposite of Doris Register. She was kind, sympathetic and could not see too well without glasses; this was good for us as we could easily scout around her.

Mr Marshall, I believe, came with the evacuees. He was a frightening man and I was never happy in his company. He had his son in the same class and we always suspected favouritism. He also had the thickest cane in the school. His journey across the classroom to the dreaded cupboard meant that some poor blighter was due for the chop: 'Oh dear, it must be me and Alan Newby.' I always felt he would have suited a concentration camp command post better. What with him and our dear friend Doris our 'life' was beyond the realms of happiness at school at times.

Miss Limmer was a war time relief mistress, she was kind and sympathetic, dispensing tea and sympathy. A great teacher and we just loved her. Two other teachers were Mrs. Nunn and Miss Mackintosh.

Teacher Marshall had a magic lanternslide. We were quite happy to sit there and watch him make a fool of himself with coloured glass. To be honest, I am not so sure he knew what he was doing, still it meant no sums and writing and we were content to sit back and watch.

Doris Register's desk was elevated on a platform, you could not sit anywhere in the room to escape her attention. She would walk to and fro on this platform, she never felt the cold as we did because the fire was next to her desk.

As with all schools, the day started off with the marking of the register. 'Yes Miss, he is ill Miss,' same old routine. Miss Register did not like to see noughts in her records, she would hold an inquiry more like the Spanish Inquisition as to why someone was not in school. If only she knew the truth and my dear friends often made excuses for my absence.

Our ink was made from powder and yes, you have guessed, our job was to make this up. Pens were of a wooden stem type with a removable nib and very scratchy to use. It was extremely difficult to get through a page in the book without a blot or terrible mess. The inkwells had to be washed once a year, not a pleasant job and this task was, of course, carried out by us boys.

Books had to be filled top to bottom, both sides of pages, inside front and rear covers with not a space wasted. Then they were inspected to see if there was still room to write more. On the front of the book was the slogan: 'Whatever is worth doing is worth doing well.' (Who thought that crazy idea up). We thought nothing was worth doing and not doing it well.

We were given a daily allocation of school milk. What a joke, fresh milk for our children, stale in summer from the heat of the sun. At the early stage of milk for all we had big urns that we boys had to measure out for each pupil. The boys knew that the bigger mug they had the more milk they would get, and often the two mug trick worked. The tap on the milk urn would often stick in the open position. Doris Register would do her usual war dance, screeching at us to turn the tap off, with the result that this made us panic and the milk run to waste. Winter saw a frozen milk situation and this grew even worse when the 1/3 of a pint bottle was introduced

Each afternoon the head girl would take the mail to the Post Office across the street at Grant's shop. Miss Register kept a few stamps in her desk drawer. Us boys would run other errands, often for other bits and pieces to be purchased from Philpott's shop. Miss Register seemed to have sympathy with old Miss Philpott; she was a nice old lady.

Church attendance was compulsory on certain days of the year and we would crocodile out of the teachers' door through the churchyard to the church. I did not mind this, my mother being a strong Christian woman, we had faith in the Good Lord. What we did not like was the visit of the parson, the Rev. Cowper Johnson, who visited the school to take religious studies. He would end up by not knowing what he was doing and of course Doris Register did not appear to want him there; she would frown behind his back.

I have to mention funerals because the corteges passed our building window weekly. We lads could always tell how popular the deceased was by the amount of flowers on the coffin and the amount of mourners that followed the coffin.

One day a week was spent on gardening on the school allotment and this was good for us boys; Dutch hoes and all, too hot some days but it was good fun. Girls did sewing out on the meadow, while we went to the allotments and did the garden, it was great fun and I enjoyed it.

Lunchtime down on the school allotment saw us boys left to our own devices. Some of the older boys remained along with us junior boys. At the stroke of midday by the church clock Teacher Marshall would be off like a shot to his liquid lunch at the 'Crown' Inn. He would sit on a window seat so that he could view the school gate with its comings and goings, leaving us boys to eat our sandwiches; there were no school dinners at that time. (If we had sandwiches).

One day, after Teacher Marshall had departed to the 'Crown,' a lad named Harry Evans was given sixpence to go to the shop to buy some wire netting seed. We needed to protect the vegetables from the rabbits that were eating garden produce. The leader of this exercise was Ivor Constance. Harry tried the first shop to no avail and the shopkeeper sent him to the second shop, and indeed to the third and fourth shops. Harry returned to the allotment just after Mr. Marshall returned; Teacher Marshall was having a head count when Harry arrived and he demanded to know where Harry had been. This, of course, led to Ivor being found out.

Ivor was frog marched to Doris Register for punishment, she was happy as she had a victim for her cane. Ivor was struck on the hand and this hurt so badly that he walked out of school to his home nearby. His mother took him to the doctor for treatment as his hand was quite bad. In the end it was all hushed up; today they would call it a lack of supervision.

And so it went on, hobnail wine from the blacksmiths, guns to shoot currants in the buns at the bakery and all sorts of jokes every day. It passed the time and broke the boredom although there was nearly always a victim of some sort.

There seems to be some discrepancy in possible attendance time at school and my actual attending. Possible attendance and actual were the same for me; I suffered from asthma at times, with a permanent cold, so it seems I had an excuse to be absent. My beloved Thorpe Abbotts featured a great deal in my absenteeism from school. In fact Thorpe Abbotts played a great part in my life from 1943-1945 and the affection that I had for the airfield then still finds a great deal of affection today.

One year I had very little schooling; although I was ill for some of the time, we just had other things to do! I would book in, disappear to the toilet, and then go off for the day. The Truant Officer on his bike would come looking for us. My mother was probably aware of my truancy but father perhaps not. They knew that if I was not at home I would be at the Taylors'.

My father acquired some POW jackets from his workplace and, as he could not afford to buy us new clothes, he thought we should wear these jackets. They were similar to Army battledress with big yellow patches. I wore one to school for two days and was then labelled 'POW' by others. I can remember Doris Register laughing at me in that jacket, we were indeed poor.

Just like today's boys fight at school, we were no different; the evacuees seemed to cause us the most problems.

Dickleburgh, Rectory Road (The Raymond Hubbard Collection)

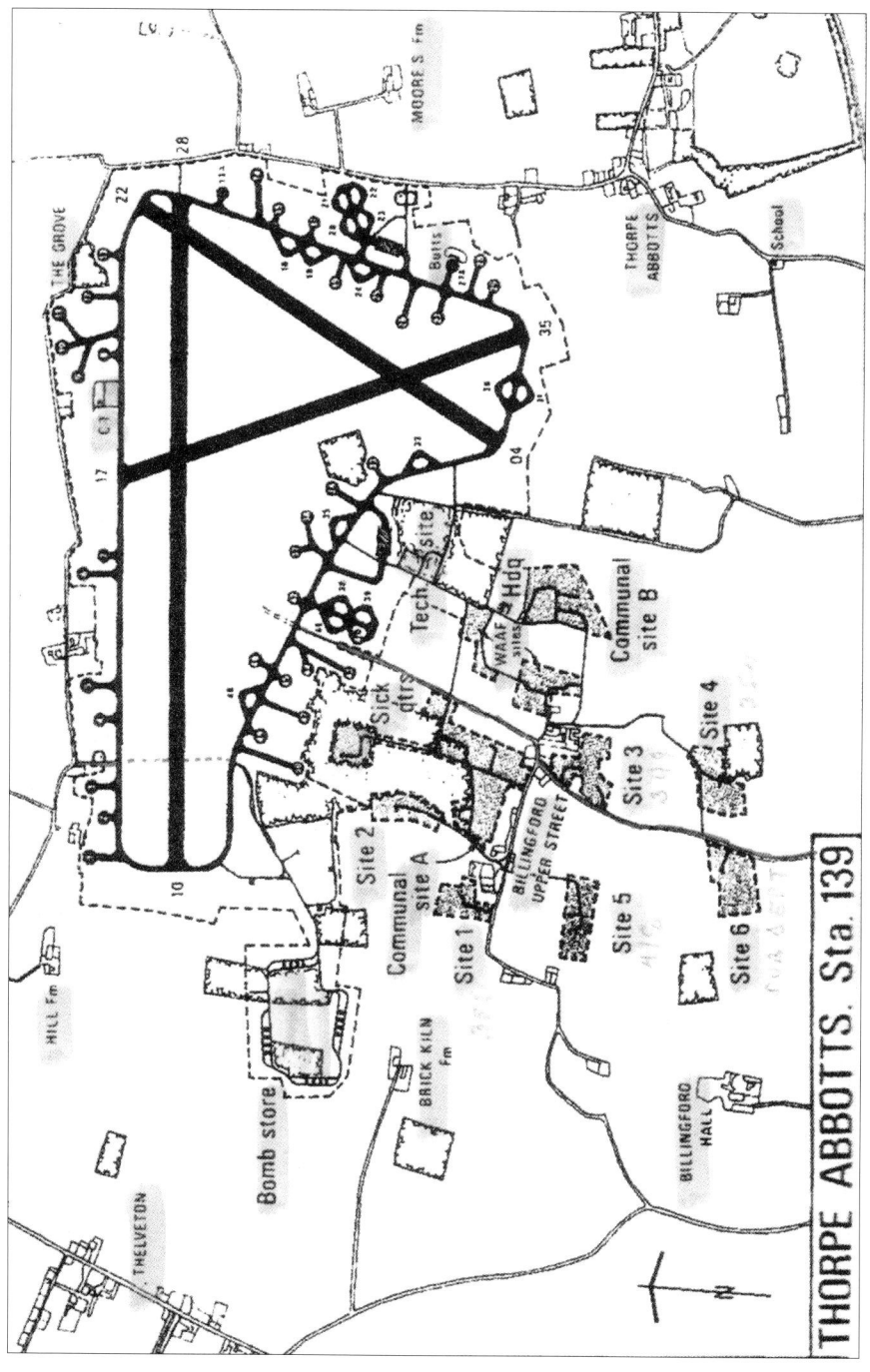

NORTHERN PERIMETER TRACK

The way in   351st Engineering   Fuel Store
The Dispersals   Billy Draper's Store
351st Tech. Supply   351st Paint Store
Control Tower site   Grove Wood   Dispersal 13
Line Telephones   Homelite Generator
100 Octane Fuel   Aircrew

Common Road started at the Manor House junction on the Ipswich Road out of Dickleburgh. There was a large piece of common land on the Dickleburgh side of Common Road and Carlton Grove, Billy Draper's chicken farm, and Hill Farm on the other. Further along was the airfield gate, close to the Taylors' house at the junction to the closed lane across to Billingford. Common Road then continued roughly parallel to the northern boundary of the airfield until, at the site of the demolished Grove Cottage, it joined the road that led directly to the eastern airfield gate and on into Thorpe Abbotts village.

The Taylors' house was technically on the airfield and therefore within the restricted area so that you had to go through the Common Road main gate to get to their house. If Billy and I wanted to go onto the airfield itself we could do this by leaving through his garden and walking to the perimeter track.

If we wanted to go to the Control Tower end we had various routes. If there were no aircraft using the perimeter we could walk along the track but, if they were taxiing round, we would go along Common Road. We had short cuts through the hedge to reach several dispersals. Near to the Control Tower there was a large opening, presumably intended as a crash entrance, but no one had got round to fitting a gate so we would walk through and up to the Tower. Further along Common Road near to Grove Wood there was another gap, where a gun emplacement was sited, so we could get to the furthest 351st Squadron dispersal. A dyke ran along a lot of Common Road on the airfield side and sometimes the short cuts could only be used by means of a small bridge or by us placing a large log across and walking over on that.

The actual concrete areas connected to the perimeter track on which the aircraft were parked were termed hardstandings. These could be several shapes although the 'frying pan' type was the most common. Together with the tent and any equipment this would form the dispersal for each aircraft. There were some fifty dispersals at Thorpe Abbotts with the four squadrons taking up a quarter of the perimeter each. The 351st Squadron was allocated Dispersals 1 to 13, strung out along the straight northern section of the perimeter. As these were the nearest to our homes and the Control Tower, we visited these often and grew to know the groundcrews serving on them; it was the 351st Squadron that 'adopted' us. The aircraft that the 100th Bomb Group flew was the Boeing B-17 Flying Fortress heavy bomber that had a crew of ten.

Although the Technical Site housed the main back up facilities, each squadron had its own engineering support near their dispersals. Beside Dispersal 2 the 351st had a Gunnery Hut. After a mission the guns were not returned to the Main Armoury but taken to the Gunnery Hut for cleaning and soon returned to the aircraft. We would ride in the back of trucks among the guns and think nothing of it. Dispersal 3 was next to the Taylors' garden.

The 351st Engineering office, a Quonset hut, was actually in the Taylors' garden. The side windows were plexiglass domes salvaged from B-17s, with desks beneath the windows. Captain Carleton's office was a small cubicle within the hut and Master Sergeant Spangler had an area for his use.

One of the airfields two main fuel stores and pumps was sited directly opposite the house on the other side of the Billingford lane. The fuel stores served as refuelling stations and we would sit up on top whilst they filled up the tankers. We knew all the refuellers and Billy's mum did their washing.

The 351st Engineering was different to our normal reception. Captain Bill Carleton was in charge but Carleton's Line Chief, Master Sergeant Spangler, ruled there. We

351st Squadron Refuelling Station (name unknown) (Sam Hurry)

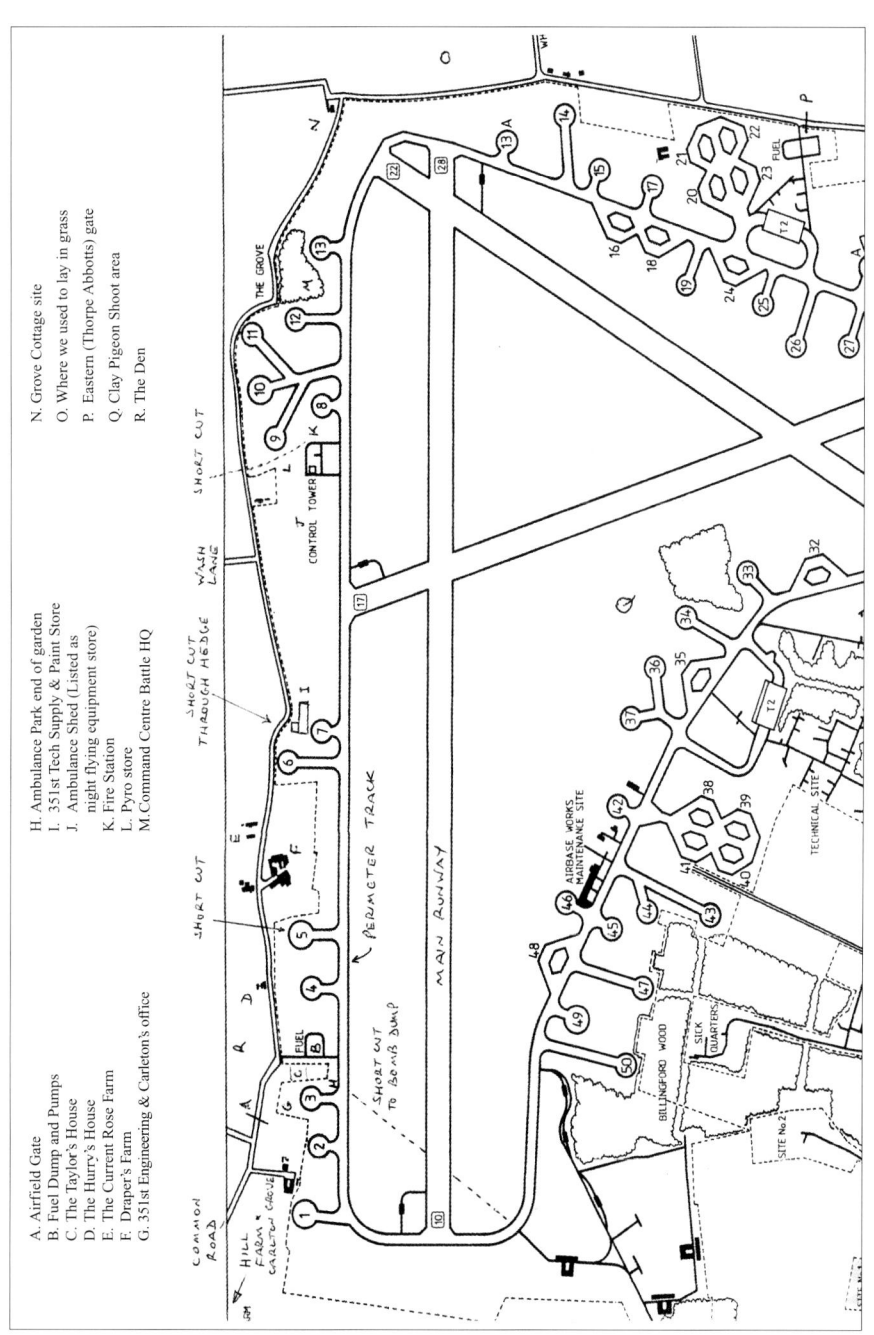

A. Airfield Gate
B. Fuel Dump and Pumps
C. The Taylor's House
D. The Hurry's House
E. The Current Rose Farm
F. Draper's Farm
G. 351st Engineering & Carleton's office

H. Ambulance Park end of garden
I. 351st Tech Supply & Paint Store
J. Ambulance Shed (Listed as night flying equipment store)
K. Fire Station
L. Pyro store
M. Command Centre Battle HQ

N. Grove Cottage site
O. Where we used to lay in grass
P. Eastern (Thorpe Abbotts) gate
Q. Clay Pigeon Shoot area
R. The Den

Thorpe Abbotts Northern Perimeter Area (100th BGMM)

351st Engineering. standing Capt. Carleton, Lt. Shand.
front l-r M/Sgts Harrison, Spangler, Lemmons, Niehaus (Sam Hurry)

were always wary of Sergeant Spangler, he did not like us boys around the aircraft but we got to know his movements and avoided him. The office had an organisational feel about it. Laundry from 351st Engineering was delivered to Billy's mother but we would go into the office when Carleton and Spangler were out and we would have a conversation with Sgt. Norton, he was more considerate to us kids. Another airman was Templeton; Mrs. Taylor looked after his washing as he was very particular in his requirements.

There were three Flight Chiefs responsible to the Line Chief, Master Sergeants Willie Harrison, Joe Niehaus and Ken Lemmons. Ken looked after four dispersals and five aircraft as two doubled up. Each B-17 had its own Crew Chief and two or three mechanics.

An ambulance was usually parked at the bottom of the Taylors' garden close to the perimeter track. Repairs to the perimeter track and side gutters were continuing all the time. Billy and I would wait until the Irish workmen had left, then walk in the wet concrete to leave our mark in history. Moving along the track, Dispersals 4 and 5 came next.

We would go up to the mechanics and ask: 'Got any gum chum?' The

The Taylors' house taken near perimeter track (100th BGMM)

frequent reply was: 'Sure have buddy, got any big sisters?'

On the dispersals we watched the riveters and armourers carrying out their duties, the bomb loading, the cleaning out, refuelling and all the usual and unusual activities that were needed to maintain a B-17. We loved to watch the groundcrew patch holes in the aircraft made through enemy action.

Us boys were required to run regular errands to obtain eggs from wherever we could get them and they were often illicitly obtained. Fry-ups would occur on the night shift in the tents beside the dispersal points, especially when the groundcrews worked through the night on major repairs to the B-17s.

They allowed us to assist in their duties and I remember helping to wash down dispersal points when the aircraft had left on a mission. The hardstanding was covered with 100 octane aviation fuel and we would be given a lighted rag to throw onto the hardstanding which immediately burst into flames, burning all the oil and grease off and leaving the hardstanding clean and ready for the aircraft to return.

Our days were highlighted when we were invited by the groundcrew to sit in the cockpits of the huge B-17s while the engines were being tested. They would shout instructions up to us to throw switches to fire the engines into life. We had been shown which switches to throw and in what order to throw them. On occasions like these the aircrew were unaware that we boys had been inside the aircraft and there were times when the groundcrew did not know that Billy and I had sat in the flight deck and seated ourselves at the controls and proceeded to win the war.

A further pleasure we had was to sit on the wings of a bomber which was being serviced at the dispersal. It was the ideal place for sunbathing, but this came to an end when a groundcrewman told us to remove our boots which were studded and could have damaged the skin of the plane. I could not take off my boots as my socks were full of holes, so for a time our sunbathing hours came to an end. Father soon rectified this by cutting to size lengths of car tyre rubber and nailing them on to my boots; fortunately Billy had rubber soles to his.

The groundcrews would take out the dinghies from their stowage on the top of the airplanes and lay them on the wings and test the blow up system. Several dinghies were obtained by local people during the war to use on local rivers as indeed were the underwing long range fuel tanks from fighters.

Another fun thing was letting off the 'Mae West' life jacket cartridges and dinghy cartridges. A small cylinder of compressed air about 4" tall was used to quickly inflate life jackets and dinghies. Every so often the cartridges would need to be replaced and we were allowed to pull the small lever to strike the cap to let them off. The groundcrew would then replace the cartridge with a new one.

Whilst we were sitting out with the groundcrew, when the bombers were airborne on a mission or practice flight, they would often play guitars and other instruments to while the time away, waiting for the return of aircraft.

One of the groundcrew could spit chewing tobacco through his teeth and shoot his spit about twelve feet or more. This fascinated us and he told us that we could achieve this by chewing some of his beech nut tobacco, which we eagerly tried. Within a few seconds we were violently sick. 'Let that be a lesson,' he said in a southern American accent.

If we obtained a full pack of sticks of gum this placed us in a very good trading position with other kids at school. The gum was of various makes, Wrigleys, Juicy Fruit, Beach Nut and Dentyne. We liked them all, and although Dentyne was considered to be a bit girlish it was still a good tradeable object. We would be given the odd Hershy Bar of chocolate, we just loved those. Usually we were given Lifesavers, which were similar to Polo Mints but all different colours. And of course, Ritz Biscuits which we ate with tinned cheese. After the war we never saw Ritz again till the 1950s, they were very good.

Early in time after the Americans arrived we were gathering water cress from the fast flowing dyke near the Taylors' residence, and further along the road at Wash Lane. The Americans loved the cress and would make sandwiches of it at the dispersals. Of course much of the water that ran over the cress came from fresh water springs, of which we always drank if we were passing, using our cupped hands to scoop up the water. It was cold water, even in summer and pure as you could find. Our water at home and Billy's house came from wells near the homes, one or two frogs were often in the water but it did not stop us from drinking it. There is nothing quite like a fresh cold drink from a deep well on a hot day. The only problem, because it was so cold, it could give you stomach cramps.

The Americans also got a taste for Norfolk apples called 'Doctor Harvey,' and we often took them some of these from Billy Draper's farm. Billy had many apple trees planted down the sides of fields and we boys were allowed to get what we needed; some were red and sweet, while Dr. Harvey's were like a golden delicious. There are still a few trees in Norfolk that are Dr. Harvey but I don't know where. Billy Draper also had apple trees at his other two farms, Hill Farm and Chapel Farm. They were well matured trees, I would think they were there before he had the farms. Anyhow, the Americans liked them, they would swap oranges for apples.

Boys will be boys and we made a den in the field near the Dickleburgh gate, not far from the Dr. Harvey's apple trees. Over time this den was equipped with various items from the airfield, including K Rations and an old chair given to us by the men.

Billy Draper's Lodge Farm was between two lots of dispersals and had the usual collection of farm buildings, that is, until one day.....

The 351st Squadron engineers, like engineers the world over, were always concerned that they might not have enough spare parts for their charges. Although stores for the B-17s were held on the Technical Site and in the squadron Tech. Supply huts, there was always the fear that a vital spare might not be readily available when needed, or take too long to acquire through official channels. They decided to improvise and Billy Draper allowed them to set up an illicit store in one of his barns on Lodge Farm.

Billy and I were running to find shelter from a storm, which were always worse then compared to those of today. We pushed at the door of the long building at Lodge Farm, it flew open and in we went. There were great heaps of stores to service airplanes, what they called 'midnight requisition.' These goods were back-up spares etc. for the 351st airplanes if they could not get the parts through normal orders. I was told later that it was often the case of a shortage of spares. Billy and I were flabbergasted to see so much stored, but of course we dare not say anything at the time. We left after the storm had finished but often returned by a window we had left unbolted, it was our drying out place after a storm.

Another port of call, behind Dispersal 7, was 351st Tech. Supply where the man in charge was Technical Sergeant Cummings. He was very good to us boys with a chocolate bar and the loan of tools to repair damage to Billy's mother's bike, although he always made us sign for them.

We often helped out by knocking packing cases to pieces or issuing tools to groundcrew. Although the groundcrews had tools on site, they needed special tools for special jobs. Tech. Supply was a loan store, piled high around it were spares of all descriptions including engines.

Often we worked in 351st Tech. Supply behind the counter. There were 13+1 clipboards hanging alongside the desks, each one with a number

Dispersal 7. 351st Tech. Supply in background.
l-r Holland, Dave, Dick Wildrick (Crew Chief) with Sammy. (Sam Hurry)

denoting the loan sheet for 1 to 13 Dispersal Points and as you handed out a special tool to do a particular job it was recorded and signed for.

Even Billy and me had to sign to loan a pair of pliers or screwdriver on the unmarked board called 'Miscellaneous.' We were only allowed to borrow if we could spell the word 'Miscellaneous.' Well, Billy wrote this down on a small piece of paper and slid it into his top pocket.

Another job we were asked to do was to keep the tortoise fires going; there was not much coke allocated so the fire did not last long.

We were always welcome at the 351st Tech. Supply, I met up with T/Sgt. Cummings after the war who then was a schoolteacher; we covered old times and he reminded me of things that I had forgotten. Sadly he has passed on.

>The record Clipboard was recorded as such:
>Pliers 8" Yankee   1 pair of
>Wire copper rolls = quantity =
>Spanner – special Ref. 089236
>However did they allow us to do this work.

One of our tasks in 351st Tech. Supply Store was to place aircraft sparking plugs in a heated cabinet. There was a cabinet about 2' 6" wide x 3' high standing on the counter. What we did was to remove spark plugs from the wax paper and place them in pre-made holes in the cabinet. There were two levels with about 50 plugs on each level. At the bottom of the cabinet on the inside was an electric light bulb which was always alight. This was to keep any possible damp out of the plugs. We seemed always to be filling the cabinet up with plugs. T/Sgt. Cummings thought we did a good job.

Behind 351st Tech. Supply was the 351st Paint Store and this was another area we were involved in. The workshop was made of packing cases and bomb boxes. We loved to get into the store, Sgt Stevens who ran the paint shop was an older man, he and us kids got along just fine. He always had time for us boys and would allow us some paint to try our artistic talents on empty crates near 351st Tech. Supply, a great man.

It was fun painting on boxes and at other times we watched the painter paint all sorts of signs. If there was a sign at Thorpe Abbotts, be sure as hell it came from the 351st Tech. Supply Paint Shop. Cycles were numbered, kitbags stencilled and aircraft nose art was created.

Probably Sgt. Stevens 351st Paint Store. (100th BG Association (USA))

Sgt. Stevens had a bicycle and a two wheeled trailer he pulled behind the bike. He would cycle off with his paint kit to paint the nose art on the B-17s or to add a bomb or swastika symbol alongside the nose art near the pilot's window. We would go into the airplane and wait for him to complete his work; a favourite spot for us was up in the nose of the B-17. There was also a Perspex repair hut near Dispersals 6 and 7. Number 6, being only some ten yards from Common Road, was one that the engineers used to blow cyclists off their machines.

Another short walk and we were at the Control Tower site. The Ambulance Shed was sited close to the Control Tower on the Lodge Farm side. Two people used to sleep inside so we did not go in there much.

The Control Tower was our second home and we spent many hours and most of our time there and in the Fire Department next door. We could always get hot coffee and food night and day. We would run errands for the Tower such as fetching flares and rockets up to the first floor and roof area. We got to know the staff as if they were our family. Sergeant 'Smokey' Follen, one of the staff at the Control Tower, worked on Air Traffic Control. He thought a great deal of us boys and was always kind.

He looked out for us, especially when officers were around or Bob Spangler was on the move. From the Control Tower we could see him in his jeep leave the 351st Squadron Engineering Office which gave us plenty of time to disappear. We just kept out of the way and moved to the Fire Department or we would often hide in the aircraft. Sometimes we got out of the rain and into the aircraft, we had a good view from the navigator's and bomb aimer's position in the nose or we sometimes sat up in the

The Tower in 1945, Grove Wood in background. (100th BGMM)

pilot's/co-pilot's seats pretending to fight the war. With the groundcrew we would sit up front, in the pilot's seat, and they would tell us which switch to throw to start the engines, this was a better education.

Often we would sit up in the Control Tower on the first floor and read the board of the aircraft allocation to missions and listen to the R/T chatting away. They did not mind us being there. Sometimes we stayed until early morning and often hitched a ride on the Ground Control chequered jeep to the end of runway.

We also had access to the 'Glasshouse' on top of the Tower roof that contained a

Sam and Margaret Ward outside Control Tower circa 1944. (Sam Hurry)

Control Tower with Pulham Airship Hangar behind. (100th BGMM)

pair of binoculars mounted on a stand. With these we could clearly see the aircraft on the far side of the airfield.

Some nights when we were in the Control Tower, doodlebugs flew to the north of us and in the clear mornings we would see V2 rockets in the eastern sky going up in Holland. The staff would not let us leave Control while all the activity was on.

Moving from the Tower to the Fire Station was an everyday occurrence and we enjoyed our time spent in both places.

Many hours were spent in the Fire Station that was sited between the Control Tower and Dispersal 8; it was always manned. These buildings were very special to us, warm in winter with an abundance of coffee and food.

The Fire staff played practical jokes on us by spraying us with foam from the front of the fire engine as we walked past. We were caught out regularly but they were good to us boys and we eventually became street-wise to this.

The Parachute Store was a Nissen hut behind the Fire Station and was not a main store but a squadron sub-store. Two people slept in here also and it held a supply of parachutes and blankets. The store always had a particular smell; I am not sure whether the parachutes were made of silk or nylon, but the smell from them was a camphor/ mothball smell.

You never forget a smell and the U.S. Army Air Force had various things that gave off its unique aroma. The smell inside a B-17 is something you never forget, it differs from a Liberator and indeed all other aircraft I have been in. 100 octane fuel smelt different to ordinary petrol. Different smells were in different buildings, the cookhouse always had that steamy water smell whereas the Red Cross building was slightly perfumed. Billets had different smells depending on what they burnt in the stoves. Coming down to earth, egg collection from Draper's stank to high heaven!

The K rations were kept in the Parachute Store and were part of the safety equipment carried on the aircraft in case of the crew having to crash land or ditch in the sea. They contained a variety of items such as emergency food, cigarettes and even matches that were capable of burning underwater.

I knew from bitter experience the taste and side effects of salt tablets, illicitly purloined from a pack of K rations, which left me drinking water from the dyke, so great was my thirst.

We boys loved to have a K ration box given to us, treating it as breakfast, dinner or supper, all good stuff. They contained biscuits, chocolates, tins of chopped ham, egg yokes, cigarettes and matches. Different meals varied in contents but whatever it was, it was welcome. I really liked the chopped ham and egg yokes, and of course loved the cigarettes.

Leslie Jefferson, Billy Taylor and Sammy on Control Tower Jeep. (Sam Hurry)

Dispersal 13 l-r Kelly, Carlson, Poukstas and Sammy. (Sam Hurry)

B-17G 'Super Rabbit' (100th BGMM)

We were also given Malted Milk tablets, these came out of ration packs, and were really good if you sucked them. Some of the nicest things from the K rations were barley sweets, and block chocolate, we could never get enough of them.

The Kerosene Store was a hut behind the Control Tower and we used to fill the cans with kerosene for use on the runway flare path.

The Pyrotechnic Store was a small brick building also sited behind the Control Tower. We used to collect flares and rockets from the store and take them to the first floor of the Tower.

There were six dispersals east of the tower, 8 to 12 quite close together, then came Grove Wood and Dispersal 13, at the end of the 351st's flight line.

Part of Grove Wood housed the ground combat troops and part contained the partially submerged Battle Headquarters which was part of our playground. In the event of invasion or any enemy action, the Battle Headquarters would have been manned with senior staff to counter the emergency. We did not visit the ground combat crew much as they slept most of the day, in a billet in the wood, because they were on duty at nights, doing guard duty and manning the half dozen or so gun emplacements. Each night one man from the Ground Combat unit would be dropped off at each aircraft for sentry duty.

Dispersal Number 13 was our favourite dispersal point. The man in charge was Staff Sergeant Poukstas. We had some very good times at No 13, we usually had our breakfast of toast and cheese there, or toast and scrambled egg.

The fire in the dispersal tent was usually red hot in winter and once toast touched the top it was done, the toast did not cook all the way through, so it had an unusual smell but a brilliant taste.

At times I admit I was more of a hindrance than a help. I had been given a cigarette lighter by a member of the groundcrew who knew that at ten years old I was already a seasoned smoker. I was now the proud owner of a Zippo type lighter and was told to fill it up with petrol from the fifty gallon tank near the hardstanding. This task I managed and in lighting up also managed to set light to the tank. The speedy actions from the groundcrew quickly put out the fire and seconds later it burst into flames again and burnt down a tent.

Speaking to Billy Taylor's widow Peggy recently, she reminded me of how late Billy and I arrived home at the Taylors' one night. We had been helping out on the 351st Line and the groundcrew needed to get this particular plane back in service for dawn, I think it was *'Super Rabbit'* on Dispersal 13. We were running errands back and forth to the 351st Tech. Supply to get special tools and other supplies and we were making coffee and cooking eggs in the tent beside the dispersal point. As small boys, time had no effect on our well being; it was after midnight that the engines of the B-17 fired into action and we could go home, after returning tools to 351st Tech. Supply. They worked through the night to get this B-17 back in service by dawn for its next day mission and this sort of thing happened all the time.

The Crew Chief had a happy-go-lucky attitude and was very easy going. This attitude sometimes rubbed off on his men and I did hear of Spangler being called out to rectify a valve that was fitted in wrongly on a B-17 at Dispersal No 13, I was not surprised.

Billy and I finally arrived home at Billy's; his father saying: 'It is too late for you to go home, so I have made you a bed on the couch.' Today this would not happen, you would be missing if you did not go home by a certain time, but then it was different, people trusted people and the world was a better place.

It was a long walk home from Dispersal 13 to No. 3 where Billy lived and we often hitched a lift in the Control Tower jeep or stopped off at the Fire Station.

Sometimes, when the men were due for a meal, they would pick us up by the scruff of our necks and hoist us into the lorries to go to the mess hall.

All over Thorpe Abbotts airfield was a line telephone system to connect squadron phones so the Workshops etc. could speak to any dispersal point tent. The telephone cables along the northern side of the airfield were hung in the hedge that bordered Common Road.

We just loved to get on these phones, I would be at Dispersal 13, Billy at Dispersal 3, and we would then dial each other to speak. The dialling was like this:

Dispersal 1 = 1 short turn of the handle
Dispersal 2 = 1 short + 1 long turn
Dispersal 3 = 1 long + 2 short

And so it changed from dispersal to dispersal and hut to hut etc. A lever on the handset allowed you to speak and then release the lever to hear. We found a way to fix our own code, it was fun - if only they knew what we got up to!

If we were some way from home and Billy wanted to give a message to his mother, we would ring from a dispersal or Tech. Supply to the Refuelling Station and one of the airmen would go through to the house, throw his cap on the table and have a cup of tea while passing on the message.

The Homelite Generator, or 'Put Put,' was a small engine on a two wheel trolley made by the Homelite Corporation of New York. It was connected to a generator on the same trolley, just like our small generators of today are. It was used to input extra electricity (DC) to support the batteries of the B-17 when starting the engines.

They were kept beside the dispersal point, quite often housed in a small bomb box home-made shelter. During engine run up we used to help out by taking the Homelite to the front of the B-17 and starting it. We could not safely reach the plug part to plug it in but with steps could do this. The cable was a heavy duty one and ribbon coated.

The procedure was to plug it in, start the generator and wait a few minutes while the generator balanced its speed according to power output. The person in the cockpit throwing the switches would start the engines one at a time and, once running, the groundcrew would remove the external power supply. We were not allowed to do this as it was close to the propellers; however as soon as they pulled the Homelite out of the way we returned it to its location beside the tent. My brother has a Homelite which he repaired and got running after importing a piston from U.S.A. with great difficulty.

I can remember the flying suits being washed in 100 octane petrol at the dispersal points. Civilians could not get petrol for any reason, yet the Americans were washing clothes in the high octane aircraft fuel. It seemed crazy at the time. They also washed the sheepskin coats in it, and it cleaned garments very well. It was not uncommon for us to wash our jackets in 100 octane as well, they dried out very quickly.

In general, the groundstaff were at Thorpe Abbotts for the duration of the war. In contrast, the aircrew came, flew their tour and usually then left the airfield. Their tour might take three to six months, depending on the weather and the military situation at the time. If they were shot down the time on the base was even shorter, of course.

The crews would be dropped off before dawn at the dispersal points and pre-flighted the airplanes so we had very little contact with them. After the mission they were collected as soon as they had landed and taken for

The Homelite Generator. (100th BGMM)

de-briefing to the Group Operations building. We did not get to know many aircrew, except by laundry bag name.

Some of the ground staff were older men, such as Sergeant Stevens of the 351st Paint Store. Many of the 351st groundcrew were in the late twenties or early thirties whereas the aircrew were a lot younger. I remember one saying he was not allowed to drive a car back home but in the Army Air Force he could fly a B-17 at eighteen.

The rubber dinghy was the key part of the survival equipment if an aircraft came down in the sea and each dinghy was equipped with a special knife. These had a large handle with a blunt ended blade to avoid causing damage to the dinghy and were attached to it by a length of cord. We boys were given one of these knives each and they were reasonably safe for us to use. We also were given a sheath knife with a blade about seven inches long, made in the U.S.A., just like a hunting knife and we would wear them on our belts all the time. They had a leathered layered handle with various colours inserted in the handle. Although they were very sharp no one bothered that we had them. We also had a compass each and always plenty of string, especially for roping on laundry!

The dinghies were provided with a coloured dye that, when released by the crew down in the sea, was an aid to their identification from the air. We were given some of this dye, I think there were three colours of yellow, green and blue, and it was very useful for showing us which way the water was flowing when we were fishing.

The Americans at Thorpe Abbotts had drums and smaller cans of purified water. The large can was about five litres and the smaller can about one litre. As soon as they were undone you could smell the tin lining which was a coated lining. Billy and I drank this water and used to carry a small can when we were out rabbiting. I must assume that the water was part of emergency rations. It tasted O.K. and while we were fishing we would put the cans (undone) into the river to cool them. Somehow we made use of materials around us and were very happy boys.

Enlisted Mens' Mess Hall used by 351st Squadron
(100th BG Association (USA))

THE LONDON TRIP

The trip I made to London was with Sgt. John D. Pearson.

The services we rendered to the Americans, such as helping with the flarepath, were recognised and appreciated by the Americans and as a thank you gesture I was treated to a day on the town. John D. Pearson and the other groundcrew at the dispersal where I helped out organised the collection to take me on a visit to London and also to buy me some new clothes.

It was late autumn when the 351st Squadron started to plan the outing, as the leaves were nearly all gone from the trees. I was told about the trip a week prior to going and mother was quite happy for me to go.

During the early weeks of preparation for the trip they had to consider the state of my clothing. I had no Sunday best and only the clothes I stood up in, no second pair of trousers, no overcoat or hat or even decent shoes/boots.

J. D. Pearson had made arrangements with the local Co-op in Diss and agreed to pay over the odds to kit me out as they had no clothing coupons. I was kitted out in due course with: 1 hat, 1 lumber jacket, 1 pair short trousers, 2 pairs socks, 2 sets of pants, 1 pair of shoes (the first I ever had because we wore boots), 1 raincoat plus a tie of scotch tartan design. It was just like Christmas when I was given the new clothes and they all fitted me correctly. I was asked to wear the clothes on a Sunday morning where they took me along the 351st Squadron Line, to photograph me with the groundcrews of each of the thirteen dispersals.

Departure to London time was 6pm on a Friday night; I duly arrived by jeep at Diss Station with J.D. and boarded the train to London. It was dark and I remember the station had no lights, only the porters with oil lamps. Once on the train and seated I can remember having a candy bar. There were other Americans on the train and it took a long time to get to London with the window blinds pulled down all the time. When we arrived at Liverpool Street Station I was in shock at the size of the station and the steam trains waiting there. Whilst coming out of the station the siren sounded and we headed for the underground.

Our accommodation was not far from Liverpool Street, it took only minutes to find it. By that time I was tired and went to bed; J.D. said he was going out for a look around and he was gone about two hours. Before bed I went to the toilet; now please remember, we did not have a flush toilet at home and whilst on Thorpe Abbotts we just did what we had to in the hedgerow. I was so fascinated by the flush toilet I flushed it several times. To me it was a wonder, and it always stuck in my mind. It impressed me more than anything that day.

We visited the zoo, waxworks, cinema and a Lyons Corner Tea House, that was just great with more knives and forks than I knew how to deal with. We toured the underground and I just loved the escalators. Late on Sunday we caught the train back to Norfolk. It was dark and cold when we got to Diss Station and a U.S.A.A.F. lorry with seats took us back to Thorpe Abbotts and then on to my home.

Monday saw me back in school and telling all my friends about the trip. It was quite a feat at my young age and of course it was wartime.

I also had the bonus of new clothes. The 351st Squadron gave me a welcome when I next visited the airfield. I thanked them all; it was money they all contributed that made possible for a young boy to extend his horizons, a truly unusual event for wartime. For information, I kept the tie until about 25 years ago. I was just lucky to have such a good time.

Watching Baseball in Rectory Meadow 1 Sam, 2 Mrs Hurry.
(100th BG Association (USA))

Dispersal Scene. (100th BGMM)

EASTERN SIDE
Hangar   Fuel Store   Firing Butts
Perimeter and Runway repairs

From Grove Wood we would walk round the perimeter to the Thorpe Abbotts side of the base. One day we were standing on the grassed area by the bend of the perimeter track when they were landing. As one of the B-17s turned the bend, which was not a sharp one, it ran down into the rain gulley; the drain top broke and the tyre burst. The pilot tried to get out by revving the engines; there was an almighty crack and the undercarriage on the left side, the one in the drain, broke.

We would call into one of the two T2 hangars, the large buildings that graced so many of the wartime airfields.

The second of the two fuel stores, and one we often visited, was located close by the east side airfield gate and the road into Thorpe Abbotts.

Not far from the hangar was the large earth rampart of the firing butts and we used to sit in the grass behind it, listening to the guns firing and the thud of the bullets.

The airfield construction gangs discovered that water was seeping in the expansion joints in the concrete perimeter track and runway. The expansion duct was filled with a fibre board. They removed this fibre and inserted liquid Bakelite that was a green colour although it soon darkened. This kept the water out of the joints but allowed flexibility. What drew Billy's and my attention was the toxic smell that it gave off when they poured it in the slot. We stood with the wind facing us so that we could smell it and the fumes gave us a heightened sense of belonging - 1943 sniffers! Nobody in those days worried about toxic smells as, indeed, us boys would also inhale a great deal of 100 octane petrol fumes.

FLYING AREA
Runway and Flight Path   Flarepath   Crash Landings   Pulham Dump   Luftwaffe   Letting off 50 Calibre   Diversions   Munster Raid   Losses   Clay Pigeon Shoot

Some days we boys would erect a sheet or two borrowed from Billy's mother to make a tent and camp out on the side of the runway. At other times it was one of our pleasures to lay on the grass at the end of the runway about 150 metres from the end and to have the aeroplanes fly over us very low indeed while they were landing and taking off. This could have been dangerous as often the airplanes were at maximum weight with fuel and bombs but it gave us a sense of belonging to the air force world, and a possible ticket to the next one! A painting depicting this scene, now on sale in the shop, came about by me talking to the artist of these events.

As we sat near the end of the runway when the B-17s took off it seemed incredible that they ever made it off the ground. The airplanes were groaning and straining due to being overweight and they rose very slowly; what a miracle to see them airborne.

Photo signed by General Doolittle for Sam. (Sam Hurry)

Some autumn evenings we would help lay the flare path for incoming planes; at that time containers that looked like watering cans were used. Our job was to sit on the tailgate of the truck and set light to the wick sticking out from the spout of each can; then we would pass the can to an airman walking beside the truck who would put it in its proper position. Every evening on flare path duty we would start clean and tidy and finish up covered in black smuts and smelling of oil. The problem was acute on foggy nights when the damp air trapped the smoke from the burning flares around us. When the flare path was laid we would be taken to the Control Tower or Ambulance Shed to wash before going to the mess for a meal. By this time it was getting late and to avoid a cycle ride home through the blackout I would stay with Billy, the better to be up bright and early for another days service on the airfield.

One time the men in the Tailors' Shop made me a small pair of overalls but, even then, they were slightly too large, and I only wore them a few times.

We saw many aircraft coming in to land on the grass beside the runway. There was the fun of sunbathing on aircraft wings, then the horror of seeing these same planes landing, riddled with shot and damaged, belly flopping across the airfield and paying no heed to runways. Our base in the Control Tower and Fire Station gave us first hand information as to what was happening.

Thorpe Abbotts where these incidents occurred was part of a huge complex organisation that was the American Eighth Air Force, it was a place of joy and sorrow, it was a place that etched itself into the heart of one English schoolboy as surely as had he been a young conscript into the United States Army Air Force.

One crash landing, in May 1944, occurred when a B-17 Pathfinder ran off the SW-NE short runway and into a ditch. If I remember, it was to the east of Grove Wood within about 500 metres of the demolished Grove Cottage site. Although I did not know this at the time, the pilot was Frank Valesh, famous in the 100th for his succession of B-17s named *'Hang The Expense.'*

On another occasion a Liberator bomber overshot the runway, landing in the local pond where me and Billy had spent pre-war days fishing. It would be another fifteen years before the contamination caused by aircraft oil and engine fluids had cleared and the pond would be fit for fishing again.

The Rushall 'Half Moon' Licensee (Sam Hurry)

Rushall 'Half Moon'. (David and Mrs. Hurry)

Rushall, 'Half Moon' at left (Raymond Hubbard Collection)

Following the completion of Thorpe Abbotts and many other airfields in East Anglia, Pulham Air Station was selected as a site for a vast dump of crashed, recovered and scrapped aircraft and the area where the scrap airplanes were stored covered about seven acres, with the aircraft stacked three to four high. A film of the time scans across what seems to be hundreds of aircraft and major parts.

A large number of the broken aircraft on the site were U.S.A.A.F. and some Americans worked on them to remove any reusable parts from the machines. The metal remaining was sent away to be re-used in the war effort although many items such as clocks, dinghies and seats were sold.

Us boys were able to get on to the Pulham dump by going through the rear grounds of the Rushall 'Half Moon' public house, kept by my Uncle Jack. It was only the case of getting over a low wire fence and crossing a ditch and we were in. Nobody ever remonstrated with us and we often spoke to the man who was in charge of the dump.

An Irishman named Tom carried out some watchman duties and there was many a whispered request behind the 'Half Moon' at night: 'Can you get me a dinghy? (or a clock......). The following night a similar meeting would take place and a dinghy would be passed over the fence.

The Germans bombed the main runway but I only saw the damage afterwards; they told me that the Americans left the gun emplacements to take cover but I don't know what truth there is in that.

Let me tell you about our hobby of letting off 50 calibre bullets. We would place this ammunition in a vice and have a very sharp nail in a long piece of wood, to allow us to stand well back. The nail would be carefully placed on the percussion cap of the bullet and Billy would strike the wood with a hammer. There was a loud bang as the bullet fired.

We had to stop this as the Taylors' shed was being holed by the bullets and Billy's father thought this was dangerous. We resorted to removing the bullet from the case, burning the explosive, and then letting the percussion cap off without the bullet.

Complete 50 calibre bullets were plentiful and were often dropped from aircraft in flight. Billy had quite a lot in his father's shed. As previously mentioned, Billy's father was a Special Constable but the least said on that matter!

Early one Sunday morning I left home to go to meet Billy and on arriving found that the taxi strip past his garden was full of R.A.F. Halifaxes. They were all lined up, maybe about fifteen. The crew or the groundcrew were cranking the engines up ready to start and about an hour later they took off. They had come in early in the morning as they could not get to their home base in Yorkshire; that was an unusual event. They had about a 6 foot long crank to turn the engines, I suppose it was like running a prop on a B-17 through to distribute the oil. It also made you think that both the British and Americans were in the same war.

One time we were sitting on the Control Tower balcony when airplanes, B-17 Fortresses and B-24 Liberators, started to land on more than one runway. It appears that other airfields were fogged out but Thorpe Abbotts was clear. There were airplanes with all the various letters of the alphabet on the tails and many Liberators. Of course in landing some ran into each other, one minute it was calm, the next airplanes were coming in from all directions. We just did not know what was happening at the time and the Fire Department was kept busy.

It was very difficult for them all to be able to park on one airfield. They had to pull the 100th's B-17s off the dispersals so that just the front wheels were left on the concrete to be able to get two more planes on. Even then all the run-ins to the dispersals had an airplane on them and the taxi track was also full.

Later that day most of the visitors had refuelled and taken off although some left the next day, I had never seen so many airplanes.

One day Billy and I were halfway down the perimeter track that runs past the Control Tower, sitting on the grass waiting for the return of the thirteen 100th Group aircraft. They had left for Munster that Sunday morning, although we did not know the target at the time.

Billy and I had spent most of the day at the Control Tower and now we stood on the perimeter track at the time they expected the force to return. Nothing happened but we continued to wait. From where we stood we could see that all was not well at the Control Tower and we could sense an atmosphere around us. We had seen the destination board in the tower and the names of thirteen aircraft that had left Thorpe Abbotts. As we waited there came the noise of engines but it was not the heavy roar of skies echoing with returning planes; only one plane appeared from behind the clouds and landed at its home base.

That was the only 100th plane to return, it had only two of its four engines running, it came in from east to west and as it was about to touch down a further engine cut out. Then, after touchdown, the remaining engine stopped. It glided along until it was opposite us when it swerved slightly and slewed to a halt. Whilst landing it was firing red flares and as it stopped it was met by the base ambulances that raced to the scene. That landing I shall never forget. The injured were brought out and wrapped in blankets and later when we walked past the camp hospital we could hear their screams. We later knew that the aircraft was named *'Royal Flush.'*

Billy Draper, the farmer, let a tree re-grow in the exact spot it stopped and what an experience that was for us two boys. Things were bad for Thorpe Abbotts that day and it showed.

Dispersals which that morning had been full of planes now stood empty, groundcrew remained beside jeeps and trucks waiting for their particular ship to return, personnel carriers still circled the perimeter waiting to collect crews from aircraft they still hoped would come home. Americans who were usually happy-go-lucky and devil-may-care in their daily lives, no longer smiled or laughed easily. There was no longer any spark of life, everyone was devastated and it was a full week before the dispersals would be occupied by replacement aircraft and a week before the mess buzzed with the enthusiasm of the new crews, things were never quite the same after that day.

In the 1980s I met up with Pappy Lewis, the co-pilot. He was being questioned about the landing and he explained it well; it happened exactly as Billy and I had said it did.

The 100th based at Thorpe Abbotts suffered heavy losses and each was felt by Billy and me; although we did not know the aircrew. We were at the runways at seven in the morning counting out the planes as they left for their bombing raids and we would be waiting when they returned, counting, waiting and hoping. Often such hopes were in vain.

Our worst days were when planes failed to return, we would sit beside the dispersal point with the groundcrew. As soon as they knew their plane was coming home they threw their hats into the air and jumped for joy. Those that did not return were very sad indeed, although some airplanes were diverted to other fields and they got to know that later.

We knew the look of men facing death each day and came to know how it was to mourn for friends who never returned.

Although the 100th lost many aircrew killed and missing in action, a considerable number were taken prisoner. When a bombardier was shot down and arrived at Stalag Luft III, a German prisoner of war camp, he supposedly asked some prisoners: 'Any of you from the Hundredth?' The response was: 'We all are.'

There was a wood between the flying area and the Technical Site hangar and just north of the wood a Clay Pigeon Shoot was sited. We did not have access to this at that time.

The snowy conditions did not prevent these 350th Squadron planes from departing. (100th BGMM)

SCHOOL PART 2

Us not so bright boys were good at maintaining the little amount of sports equipment we had, so we were useful after all! It was a good job to have complete freedom in the cloakroom while others were allowed to read. Friday afternoons was 'bring a book time' or sewing and knitting for the girls; as we had no books our task was working on the sports equipment.

The War affected the school in many ways. Cod liver oil, Bengers Food, Malt extract and Virol were provided to some of the children; how come I never had these things. Most youngsters did, I suppose they lacked something or other. They were brought into the classroom with Doris Register on the spooning end of the business, she was always keen to issue out the rations.

No sweets in the shop this week, our dear friend Richard Chenery, who was always good to us, has sweets all the time; perhaps it is because his granny keeps the shop.

Not much food at home, and remember there were no school dinners, so every crust was consumed. Salvage time saw us collecting for the war effort, there was a National Savings 'Penny a week' bank which was all administered by, yes, our dear friend Doris Register. I was given a certificate in helping the War Effort Commonwealth Day Celebrations.

Sometimes we would find the school was closed again, the Army were using it as barracks. This was great news, we could sit around on the street corner and watch the Army go by in tanks and other vehicles, or visit my beloved Thorpe Abbotts. At other times the school was used as a social centre for the village.

Police Constable Fowler came in to tell us about 'Butterfly Bombs' and we did not like him coming into school for fear that he would arrest us for laughing or stealing turnips to help out the food rations. Thorpe Abbotts airfield was under construction and saw me absent from school more times than I can remember. Shutters were made for the windows in the school and tape placed across the glass. The bombing of Pulham Air Station rocked the classroom and Teacher Marshall said that it was thunder; but we knew different, we were not frightened, just inquisitive.

Air raid practice saw us all in the Air Raid Shelter on the playing field. These were constructed of a dug-out trench with a lorry chassis on top, then with galvanised sheeting and soil on top of that. There were two rows of seating the length of the shelter. Not bad down there, dark and a cuddle with the girls, very cold in winter. Gas masks were always carried, the infants had the Mickey Mouse type. Tests were carried out from time to time and it was great fun doing lessons in gas masks. The war dragged on and on and we were continually interrupted by the school being used as a barracks. We occasionally had lessons in the Baptist Chapel in case the school had to be evacuated.

The bakehouse were selling 'Hot Buns' (minus the currants) for one penny so we had a hot bun before school. The war effort seemed to dominate our life at school and the continued pull of my beloved Thorpe Abbotts saw Billy Taylor and me frequently on the airfield. There somehow seems to be a vacancy in my schooling during the war, I wonder why. The end of the war saw celebrations and the church bells rang again.

Summer time brought cricket and rounders; that's a girls game rounders, we would fight shy of that. Football was played but there were no football boots, no spare ball and the one we had was patched and sewn with string. Cricket bats kept falling apart and there was no money to buy new ones; we were happy just to be in the fresh air. Doris would concentrate her efforts on the girls, so us boys would gradually disappear, she would dismiss the class from the playing field so it meant that she never really knew if we were all there.

Regretfully, not enough outings took place. We had more outings by belonging to the Sunday School at the Chapel than we did through the school but, as sure as the sun rises, we would inevitably go off to Yarmouth for a day out, with the kindest help from Farmer Draper.

Results time would come round, famous names were Newby and Hurry, we both held the position of near bottom of the class. We always said it was to hold the others up top, some sort of sacrificial cows I suppose. We never had a chance to gain a position upwards, we were ignored and not encouraged as indeed so many more like us.

Prize Giving was the usual stuff, bibles, more bibles, a never ending supply of bibles, they must have had a secret store somewhere. They were not for me though, I never received a prize, it never really interested me. However, the parson knew where to come when he needed help with the churchyard or in the church, yes us boys.

We were aware that some were 'The Privileged.' Some pupils went on to grammar school either by scholarship or having money and this we felt was an unfair way of gaining a better start to life. At that time we had some bitterness towards the system that allowed money to buy an education. As I have already said, we had nothing but happiness and a good home. I often feel that today people have everything but they lack happiness.

We also knew others were even less fortunate. Some pupils whose fathers did not work were supported by the parish and often their children were open to ridicule, I did not like this form of punishment to fellow pupils and would not associate myself with it.

The summer holidays and harvest time was the most popular time of the year with the long days of the double summer time. Away to the fields and a job on Draper's farm, equipped with a special size pitchfork and freedom from the schoolroom. We had six to eight weeks depending on the harvest, how lovely to drink beer with the men and spit and swear a little. We were beyond the call of Miss Register and her orders to: 'Do this', 'Do that', 'Not now', 'You are late', 'Wake up boy', 'You are lazy', 'Sheep's head', 'Idiots', the vocabulary of that woman was enormous in finding some way of condemning us to hell or beyond.

After the holidays it was a return to familiar surroundings. Can't move up any higher in the classes, same place on return from the holiday, same desk, same class, except during our absence the school was scrubbed clean by the cracked and rough hands of my mother and others like her.

In early September Mr Snelling Senior, 'the Apple Man,' would bring baskets of apples and throw them on the meadow for us to eat, sometimes we were given these in July. We looked forward to his visit, a very kind man; his daughter and my aunt, Mrs W. Wells lived in Slate Cottage, Rectory Road in Dickleburgh.

Story time, some days we were allowed to listen to the radio. The accumulator was charged up of course by none other than my brother who worked at the mill. I liked listening to the radio, it was very relaxing and I often fell asleep. I was too tired to concentrate due to work before school and more work after school.

For a few fleeting hours we were able to go along with the animal hunt by playing truant. We loved to follow the hunt through the fields, but alas, later on we were often caught by the Truant Officer. There were one or two hunts near the end of the war, but not many until after the end of hostilities.

Here we go again, it is concert time, all the best parts in the school plays go to the favourites. Some of us boys were stage hands, some were crowd clappers. I did get two parts, a Wiseman and a ventriloquist's dummy; I think the latter one suited me better. Hard work weeks ahead of the school concert saw us far too long in school premises. Well it was probably worth it as the Christmas party was near.

The school was heated by large open fires, not too good or efficient; often they would go out and would have to be relit. Overcoats were often worn in class and in the mornings I have seen ink frozen in the inkwells. (Just remembered, I had no overcoat!).

We all liked Christmas as it meant holidays and decorations, we had nothing, nor did we get anything, but we were happy and that meant a great deal. Christmas was time to go off on the snow plough, time to put our books away (what books). We had very few text books, those that we had were outdated, tattered and best described as paper aeroplanes. One book was often shared between three of us.

The village library was housed in the school. It contained perhaps one hundred books at the most, not good for us kids. The adults would come in after school for their library books. This was again run by no other than our dear good headmistress, Doris Register, who would have one girl stop late to help with the tickets and filing the returned books. A different woman, Miss Register, when she was dealing with adults. If only they knew the truth. Perhaps she used the library system as a Parent Teacher Association, who knows what that woman had in her mind.

After the war on Mondays we older boys would go off to Diss for carpentry although this was not much use to me, I was never any good with wood. As the girls did cookery, the Eduction Committee must have thought all boys to be carpenters and all girls cooks; not much thought or planning went into the work and often it was a wasted journey. Still it allowed us out of school and into Diss for some independence.

I deserted school, leaving before my time. A boy was needed to lead the horse in the bean field, so with cold tea and sandwiches I set out to earn my fortune (what fortune), before I was officially allowed to leave. It was hard work, the days were long and filled with utter exhaustion, but there were a few pence in my pocket.

WESTERN SIDE

Poaching   Bomb Dump   The Bomb Dump Fire   Hospital   John Laing Compound   Water Tower

One time we were out poaching, to the Hill Farm side of Dispersal 1, not far from Billy's, when up jumped a pheasant. Billy shot the bird and I was sent to pick it up. In the distance I could see a gamekeeper on his bike heading in our direction. It was getting dark so we had to do a quick retreat, running across the airfield to hide in a dyke. We had no dog with us at that time. We could see the gamekeeper pick up the bird and hear him cursing the 'Bloody Yanks' for shooting a pheasant. We were at the bottom of the dyke with water up to our necks with the keeper standing above us. As it was dark he did not see us but was swearing all the time about the 'Bloody Yanks.' After a while I was sent out to scout around to see if he had gone. We made it back home to tell Billy's mother that the pipe came off a water pump as we were watching a manhole being pumped out. A big drying session followed and we had to return the next day to retrieve the gun from the dyke. This was one of many of our attempts to avoid the keeper.

We often saw jeeps with guns covered with overalls so the Americans could take pot shots at the pheasants; after all, they were shooting back in the States with no restrictions

If we wanted to go to the western part of the airfield on leaving Billy's garden we would cross the perimeter track, take a short cut across the main runway, and cut off towards the Bomb Dump.

I must mention our bomb dump travels; it was good for rabbiting, strawberries, and sitting out in the sun on the bombs. We would cadge a lift on the loaded or unloaded trolleys to distant parts of the airfield. In July we would collect our fill of wild strawberries from the bomb dump.

Moments of danger and alarm were tempered by lighter moments. I remember a mid-air collision between two aircraft directly over the airfield which caused one of the planes to crash on the bomb dump in the south west corner. An unofficial evacuation ensued with servicemen commandeering bicycles and heading at high speed away from the crash site; they were leaving Thorpe Abbotts by every possible means. Some personnel used the incident as the excuse for some unofficial leave, and during the confusion managed to leave the airfield. The story was told of a GI spotted locally pushing a bicycle at the double along the lanes; when asked why he wasn't riding it he replied that he just hadn't had the time to get on it. Fortunately for all the personnel the wreckage, when it fell, missed the high explosive store landing instead on the incendiary dump; by night the fires were under control and a near disaster had been narrowly averted.

We were not allowed on the airfield that day; the Military Police were evacuating the base. They told Mrs Taylor, Billy's mother, to vacate her house because of the possible explosions but she soon told them off saying: 'The Germans can't get me out and neither are you.' The locals living nearby would not move either.

Brick Kiln Farm was situated not far from the bomb dump and we knew the family who lived there.

The Base Hospital was in a clearing in the woods and we would pass this on our way to fishing and would stop and speak to the Americans sitting outside in the sun during summer. We did receive First Aid occasionally from the hospital, they were good to us boys.

John Laing & Son Ltd. was the main contractor for Thorpe Abbotts and they built the airfield, keeping a presence on site during its operational use. We would stop off at the John Laing Airfield Compound and say 'hello' and get a strong cup of tea each from the civilian workers. The compound was on the corner of the road leading up to the hospital.

We would visit one of the two water towers which were provided with inspection ladders up to the top – ideal for boys who were good at climbing!

COMMUNAL SITE 1 - THE BILLINGFORD SIDE
Mess Halls   Post Exchange   Cinema   Red Cross
Dickleburgh and Pub   The Cycle Saga
Blast Shelters

There were two 'Communal Sites' on the airfield that included the Mess Halls and various group activities. There were eight other 'Sites' that provided accommodation for the officers and other ranks.

We used to eat quite often in the Communal Site 1 Airmens' Mess Hall, the 'Chow Hall,' which was used by the 351st Squadron and was close to their accommodation area on Site 1. An airman would sometimes take a bone to Billy's dog, waiting patiently outside.

If we passed the Post Exchange, the 'PX', they would give us sweets and chocolate, we never had to ask for anything. We just could not get enough of Lifesavers, similar to today's Polo sweets; they were good and quite tradeable with other lads. I did have difficulty of working out the word candy, not a familiar English word at the time.

Sometimes, after visiting the Mess Hall, we would make use of the Airmens' Latrine and the Airmens' Shower and Ablution Block. A civilian

The Red Cross Hut. (100th BG Association (USA))

59

The Red Cross Library. (100th BG Association (USA))

was employed to keep the shower house fire going. The cookhouse had water outside for cleaning the airmens' cutlery (irons), with hot water for washing and cold for rinsing.

We only went to the camp cinema two or three times, they had a strict check on the door that was something to do with regulations. It was a large Nissen hut with the projector room elevated at one end of the hut, I can't remember if they had to pay to go in but it always seemed busy.

We went into the Red Cross Hut for refreshments and games, a lad from Dickleburgh worked there. Christmas Parties were held in the Red Cross building. I recall all the local children looking at the presents stacked high near the Christmas tree, amongst these was a very large package, in fact the biggest parcel. The other children viewed this hoping this was theirs, but it was earmarked for me, a snooker table and you can imagine my happiness with such a gift.

The Red Cross was next to the Mess Hall where we used to eat quite often, a stone's throw from the PX and the cinema.

Some service women of the American Red Cross worked in the Red Cross building and either slept there or in their quarters nearby. A few nurses who worked in the hospital also used these quarters although I can only remember seeing four or five women on the base at any one time.

The local pubs in the area opened at 7.15 pm but, in the village of Dickleburgh the 'Crown' and the 'King's Head' were invariably closed at 8.00 pm, the Americans had drunk the places dry. Other local hostelries were equally popular, including the 'Half Moon' at Rushall and, favoured by the 351st Line crews, the 'Ram' at Tivetshall.

Sometimes we were asked to fetch bread for toasting in the dispersal tent from Dickleburgh Bakery. There was never any problem to obtain such bread as Billy Draper's brother ran the village bakery and indeed we were asked to get light bulbs from Saunders at Dickleburgh, again no problem, the Drapers' and Saunders were friends.

As young boys, both Billy and I had wondered how there were so many cycles around the airfield. We discovered the source of such vast numbers of cycles. At the Thorpe Abbotts pub there was a cycle repair workshop, Valiants Cycles, and hundreds of cycles were stored there. It was said the owner would go out at night and collect the cycles that the Americans left in the hedgerows after coming out of the pub. He would take them back to the workshop, re-paint them and sell them again. A refurbished bike made good money and the Americans did not know where they had left their bikes. There were quite a few American made bikes on the base but I don't think those were involved with re-cycling (no pun intended!) as they were fitted with a back pedal brake and had a serial number that was registered with the Provost Marshall.

Most of the bikes were locally obtained in the first place from the seller at Thorpe Abbotts, some however came from Brockdish, the next village. My brother worked there after the war repairing cycles and he said there was still a big store of ex-Army bikes at Brockdish.

There were many blast shelters on the airfield on the social and domestic sites. Many a time we were ushered into the blast shelters, a double corridor of 5' to 6' walls. When the Germans bombed the runway the ground gunners were very active. The gas rattles were situated out at the front of some of the buildings; we often got to turn the handle and watch the result. (One of the shelters on this site is still there).

The Mission Fair came to Thorpe Abbotts at the time of the 200 mission party. I can't remember much about this except that it was the first time we had coke and ice cream, but we did not go on any fairground rides.

CRASHES

The Draper's barn crash by Valesh, the Dickleburgh Rectory Meadow crash, the one in Scole Nursing Home woods and the Thelveton crash are just a few of the twenty or thirty crashes that we witnessed and the intense heat and exploding cartridges were felt and heard by us. Burning, crashed aircraft have a smell that is so different to anything else.

One day three aircrew and two American Red Cross girls set out for a joy-ride in a B-17. Just before take-off there was a serious vibration that caused the bomber to swing to the right and off the runway. It hit two trees and careered into Lodge Farm. The plane, ironically named *'Hang the Expense'*, was written off and Billy Draper's bull in a farm shed that was demolished by the impact was killed. Fortunately there was no loss of human life.

I have kept quiet about the Dickleburgh Rectory Meadow Crash to date as there was always someone who said they were there. This was the first crash suffered by the 100th at Thorpe Abbotts. My brother Derek, Richard Baker, me and one other which I think was Bernie Stone, were out of school and just about to go into the Rectory Meadow near to Mrs Seaman's house when this great big airplane came roaring across the searchlight field and crashed into the trees in Rectory Meadow. It burst into flames and there were injuries amongst its crew. We did not stop to look but ran in the opposite direction for fear of bombs. I have indeed heard many a tale about this crash, but have kept quiet, people do romance so.

Once Billy got his mother's bike moving, with me on the handlebars, we could respond pretty quickly to any event as we knew all the short cuts. We did not see the aircraft crash in the grounds of Scole Nursing Home but we cut through the Bomb Dump and past Brick Kiln Farm to get to the site. The bomber had taken off the tops of the trees and what remained of the aircraft and the trees were burning when we arrived. Some locals were standing nearby watching but the ambulance and fire trucks were still on their way.

The crash on the Bomb Dump I saw but only from a distance though. Another crash at Billingford was quite severe, Billy and I saw this go down but not close enough to see the details.

The worst crash we saw was on the outskirts of Thelveton. We were out rabbiting, and what else we could get, when this B-17 came roaring over our heads. We dived into the ditch, the next thing there were flames that seemed all around us and people screaming. It was there that I saw my first dead American with the cogs from an aircraft ball turret embedded in him. It was a great shock to Billy and me, it changed our lives to an extent and afterwards we viewed all crashes with a frightened feeling. We witnessed many crashes, there are far too many to write the details down here.

The aircraft or the wreckage from the crash sites was collected up and loaded onto long Queen Mary lorries. They were then mostly taken to Thorpe Abbotts Base and the Hangar Queen area by the hangar on the Technical Site. Later they were taken on to Pulham Air Station, 53 M.U., for salvage. The Queen Mary lorries often had a problem getting round the Dickleburgh street corner on the way to Pulham. We would watch them trying to turn the corner with those very long trucks, sometimes we would hitch a lift on them, the R.A.F./civilian people did not mind this.

Winter scene in the Technical Training Area (100th BGMM)

TECHNICAL SITE
Hangar   Hangar Queen   Water Tower   Radio Workshop
Chapel   Norden Building   Provost Marshall   Mess Hall
Blister Hangar   Link Trainer   Bomb Aimer Training
Parachute Packing   Motor Transport Section

Not far from the southernmost of the two hangars was the Technical Site which is where we spent hours and hours. We did not know many people there, but did know some in the Motor Transport Section and the Radio Repair Shops. We also got to know the engineer who ran one of the two power plants which were generators driven by McLaren heavy oil engines. After the war these were sold on to the Arabs to help pump oil and my brother helped to remove them from the engine sheds.

From the Radio Workshops we would wander into the big hangar to watch them repairing the airplanes, huge buildings to us boys.

A B-17 that was considered unfit to be restored to flying condition became the current Hangar Queen. Any re-usable parts would be removed for other aircraft and the machine gradually cannibalised until there was nothing more to remove. At that point the aircraft would be taken to the dump and another damaged aircraft would take its place. We loved to roam through the B-17 that was laid out over two half circle supports.

The second Water Tower was next to the T2 and from the hangar we would go and speak to the civilian man who ran the water pumps for fresh water. Little did he know that soon afterwards we would be up on top of his tanks, sitting in the sun.

Some rainy days we would find ourselves in the Radio Workshops that maintained radio and other equipment. We would sit there with the Americans, listening and watching repairs being made and the testing of various radios, quite a nice place to be. We never got interrupted and again always a drink and eats.

We often sat outside the Chapel which to my memory was always busy. This was next to a Mess Hall and Ration Store, not far from the Group Operations Building.

A few hundred yards further up the road from the Chapel was this special compound and building which housed the Norden bombsights, although we did not know this at the time.

Another event in our young lives was the enforced visit to the Provost

Marshall's office. At one time there was trouble from the older village lads coming to the base stealing from the buildings. For a while everyone was implicated. The Provost rounded all the lads and those about there at the time and took us all to the Provost Office. Very frightening indeed; in the end they caught some older men and youths and if I remember us boys were banned for three weeks being on base, but that time went quickly and we really did not stop going, we just kept low.

We had food quite often in the Mess Hall. We were allowed to do just what we wanted. After my initial visit, I did not go much on the system of all main food and sweet on the same plate or often, mess cans. One can for food, one can for coffee. I love both and know how lucky we were to have such freedom and fun.

As mentioned, there were two main Mess Halls at Thorpe Abbotts, apart from the Sergeants' Messes and Officers' Club.

The Blister or Blitz Hangar was a large, very large, Nissen Hut with the traditional curved sides of these huts. Inside the building various types of gunnery training were carried out. Yes, we did the practice just as they did, including the ball turret training. I must say at this point, whilst we were in this area we had to go carefully as the Provost Marshall's office was next door.

We would go into the Link Trainer building and they would allow us to sit in a Link Trainer and run it up. Billy and I would sit in the yellow painted trainers and believe we were fighting the war.

The Bomb Aimers' Training Unit was a very tall building for the next type of training. For this we had to climb a makeshift ladder/stairway as the position of the trainee was way above ground level. This was probably about 60 feet up and we would lay in the position and practice dropping bombs on a moving map type affair. Quite interesting, we did this several times.

The main parachute packing shop was another tall building, so that the parachutes could be fully extended. They were then laid out on long tables for packing by skilled personnel.

There was a vehicle ramp in the motor vehicle section that we would ride up and come down the other side with me on the handlebars of Billy's mother's bike. One time Billy, speeding up the ramp, failed to notice that the brickwork slope at the far end had broken off. I shouted to Billy but as I was on the handlebars he could not see anything and of course, with certainty, we rolled off the end of the broken ramp to make a mess of his mother's bike. I'm pretty sure that I remember the M.T. Section repairing the bike. We needed to get home as Billy's mother needed the bike to go to a Whist Drive at Billingford; it did not bear thinking about. That time the bike was repaired and she did not notice the repairs done on her cycle, thanks to the chaps in the M.T. Section. They had petrol pumps and workshops on site, there were around ten or so who worked there.

ADMINISTRATION SITE
Group Headquarters   Group Operations
Commanding Officer

We would cut through the site on our journeys across the airfield on our way between the Technical Site and the Communal Site 2 and the Sewage Works area. Although this was the heart of the base, we would walk past Group Headquarters and Group Operations without being accosted. We might be asked: 'Where are you boys going?' but this would often result in the offer of a lift in a vehicle or on a cycle crossbar. The Commanding Officer's quarters were on Communal Site 2.

Some aircrew officers had their accommodation on the W.A.A.F. site (this was named from the R.A.F. planning days and no women lived there), and they would speak to us.

SOUTHERN AREA

The Sewer Works was at the southern extremity of the base, not far from the A143 road that connected Diss to Great Yarmouth. The person who ran this was a civilian and we would often visit his small concrete gate house; he would allow us into the area for rabbiting and other illicit poaching.

Thorpe Abbotts was a place of plentiful supply of rabbits, we would take the dogs and guns and proceed via the Bomb Dump to the Sewage Works at the far side of the airfield. That's where we got the biggest and best rabbits and pheasants' eggs when in season. Usually I went home with two rabbits, Billy three or four to feed the ferrets. Yes, we always took the ferrets carried in Billy's shirt.

DEPARTURE

Our lives were devastated, shattered, nothing to belong to but our memories, we were left with the whole airfield of Thorpe Abbotts. The silence was unnerving, the skylarks could be seen and heard in the air, we had not noticed these before, it was only the silence that attracted our attention to them although they existed during the war.

The atmosphere was ghostly, buildings with doors left open, some furniture still in place, curtains blowing in the wind, ashes in the tortoise stoves, magazines on the floor, roadways deserted, the hospital empty, nothing remained that was alive. Water ran from some taps, equipment was still in some buildings, electric generators were silent, no bombs in the bomb dump, empty racks in the PX, the sewerage farm still working, a few civilians listing, taking notes, fire buckets, gas rattles still stood in place.

Daily we visited our old haunts, the Control Tower, the Fire Station where a few weeks earlier we had enjoyed coffee and eggs. All was silent, we walked the whole airfield hoping we were wrong and that they would be back; alas it was not to be, realization eventually came but still we visited our beloved Thorpe Abbotts.

At night Thorpe Abbotts brought about an even ghostlier situation, many nights we ventured on to the airfield, huts silhouetted against the moonlight, the experience of the phantom B-17 charging down the main runway, (pure imagination, who knows?).

Barracks that were alive a few weeks previously stood empty, the owls hooting in the woods, the occasional window banging in the breeze, it was the most difficult period of our young lives to adjust to an emptiness that was not of our making. Did we ever adjust?

The seasons came and went, Thorpe Abbotts started to deteriorate, wildlife became abundant, wild strawberries grew again in the bomb dump, grassland was torn up and returned to farming, we were alone, very much alone as our beloved Thorpe Abbotts slipped into history.

> *We searched the sky in all directions*
> *Hoping that our thoughts were wrong*
> *No sound was heard, no distraction*
> *No dream was dreamt for so long*
> *The airfield was empty, devoid of life*
> *A ghostliness existed, it hung in the air*
> *Nothing happened after the strife*
> *Buildings, roadways, runways, no funfair*
> *For they had gone across the sea*
> *We know not why, both Billy and me.*

When the Americans pulled out in December 1945 I was nearly twelve years old. We had missed much of our formal schooling, yet living on the doorstep of an operational airfield and developing close and lasting friendships with those stationed there had given a broader education than any classroom could offer.

Eleanor Hurry outside 13 Rectory Road, circa 1945 (Sam Hurry)

POST-WAR

After they had left Thorpe Abbotts we would go to the Water Tower and into the pump house, turn the pump wheel and raise fresh water. The tanks had been emptied, but the wells to both pumps were still there; also the farmer used to run the pump with a donkey engine to supply water for his stock.

I spoke recently with the son of the man who ran the supply, a Mr. Catchpole. What was interesting was that the description I gave Mr Catchpole Junior was identical to what his father had told him.

Post-war, the Clay Pigeon Shoot became our joy and pride - to think we were able to shoot at clays! It was hard for me to load the machine which sprung the skeet. Billy always fired the gun while I just loved the skeet thrower. This equipment was in place long after they had left with boxes and boxes of clays.

The Tower filled with straw 1952.
(Sam Hurry)

The cartridges we found there also fitted Billy's 12 bore shot gun, so it was free ammunition for us shooting rabbits. Often live ammunition was left lying around, they did not care that much. The cartridges were not always in the best condition and Billy used to put them on his mantle over the fire to dry out. (Phew!)

When the war was over the hospital turned into a ghostly place and we avoided it. The dogs would stop and not go through the grounds. Billy was very wary of the hospital. It was the first building to be pulled down and cleared, I know not why, as the land was not needed and it was surrounded by trees. We came back from fishing one night, quite late, past the site of the hospital and we had quite a fright as there appeared to be screaming and several owls flying about. I have not seen to this day such an abundance of owls in one place; one of life's mysteries.

The dogs would not go in some buildings but would cower outside as if there were other presences. This often happened; the hospital site was one, the Bomb Dump buildings and the Group Operations building were others; yet they happily slept in the Sewage Site building. Often the dogs had a fit and we just had to wait for them to recover, we hardly ever went out without the dogs or guns.

The hangars were used to store Navy mines, then for about three years they were used by the Ministry of Food and Fisheries to store corn. Thousands of rats contaminated the stores and I think it was all destroyed. The hangars were taken down and sold during the 1950s.

Billy and I collected many Pin-up pictures, torn from the 'Sad Sack Shack' and from various billets. It did not last long as the requirement was looming up for him to join the forces for his National Service.

Post-war the government had the grassland torn up and gyrotilled the soil which threw plenty of flints and stones up to the surface. The Ministry of Agriculture operated six Fowler Gyrotiller Diesel Rotary Ploughs from about 1934. These giant 170 hp machines ploughed the earth to a depth of two feet. After that we helped to clear the land by stone picking for which we were paid 3d per bushel. Many other lads and girls did the same, it was indeed hard work, two of us trying to carry a bushel of stones.

In the Control Tower Billy and I would find boxes of tools, radios and all sorts of merchandise, even rubber dinghies and K rations in some of the huts.

Later on the Control Tower was used first to store straw and then to house pigs. Billy Draper kept quite a few pigs in there.

On cold days we would light a fire in the stove in one of the huts as there was plenty of scrap wood around and, indeed, coke to burn. The dogs would curl up around the fire and we would get the top of the stove red hot, with our clothes steaming from being wet.

I don't think I have ever experienced such silences as there were at Thorpe Abbotts after the Americans went home. During the day you could hear the Navy working, storing the mines, but that was all. Oh, so quiet.

The first Quanset Hut on the 351st Line was used by the Dickleburgh Scouts, of which I was a member. Raymond Hubbard and Alan Newby were both in the Scouts and on one occasion we travelled by train to a large Scout rally at Sandringham, passing through, or changing trains at Kings Lynn.

The 351st Engineering office of Bill Carleton was used as a wood store, but not for long. The 351st Tech. Supply hut remained empty.

Living accommodation on Site 6 became housing, modified by Depwade

Rural District Council, and some of the other buildings were also converted as there was a housing shortage. As the Council built more council houses, so the airfield huts were vacated, but some were occupied for several years. We used to join up with the kids who lived in the huts.

Many of the buildings were used by farmers to store machinery, excepting those near the Bomb Dump which remained empty. Some buildings were torn down and removed. Cables and piping were stripped out of some buildings through theft and, indeed, some electrical cables were pulled out of pipes by using lorries. What was left in some buildings was then looted; people were leaving Thorpe Abbotts with loaded handcarts. I think the police tried to stop this but without much effect.

After the work in the bean field came to an end I went to work in the village bakery and later attended Norwich City College. After that I joined the R.A.F. for three years, served in Germany and was demobbed in February 1955.

Until July 1955 I worked at Ipswich and then joined a multiple national company. I was promoted to Retail Manager and managed fifty five retail outlets, finally settling at Kings Lynn.

In 1964 I married Jane, who was a telephonist, and we had two sons, Simon and Robert.

After twenty seven years of training managers and running a shop, I left to become a lecturer at the local college. Gaining my teacher's qualifications, and indeed other qualifications, produced a position in a job that I liked. After a while I was running a small department teaching business studies and logistics, this was a world that well suited me.

All you pupils that read this, take note. You will never have another chance like the one you have at present, work hard, play hard and the world is yours for the taking. Learn all you can while you are young, you will need it when you are older. Childhood is but a fleeting moment in your life, adulthood is a longer fleeting moment. Knowledge is the most valuable asset you will have, other than health and happiness

After Billy joined the Navy he went for training at *H.M.S. Ganges* and when he came back on leave he looked older and fitter. He came home from Portsmouth and returned there to join *H.M.S. Belfast* to go to Korea. Billy's ship was a Second World War cruiser that provided fire support for the United Nations forces during the Korean War.

I don't think he had a very good time out there. He did write occasionally but never about the war, only about when he would come back and the plans he made before going to join *H.M.S. Belfast*. He met Peggy, his wife to be, and they were well matched. Between me going in the Air Force and Billy serving his naval time I would go up to the Taylors' and sit and talk to his mother and father and his brother George. A tear would often come into his mother's eye; *H.M.S. Belfast* was indeed in active waters and his family were often talking about him.

I can't say I saw much of Peggy, she probably visited the Taylors when I was not there. It was a shock to me, him going off to join the Navy, Billy was sorely missed. After his final return home he would not talk about his experiences and he and Peggy made their home together; by that time I was in the Air Force. Strange how it all happens, I know my mother piped her eyes when each of us brothers left home for the Air Force.

Later Billy worked in a Builders' yard, spent some time as a bus driver but lost his job and became a Water Bailiff. One of the biggest poachers, although he was the Water Bailiff, Billy would catch fish in his lunch hours.

Billy Taylor in uniform
(Peggy Taylor)

POST WAR U.S.A.

The 100th moved out of Thorpe Abbotts during the latter months of 1945 and the personnel returned to the U.S.A. There, the resumption of normal life, finding work, training for careers, starting businesses, getting married and raising families preoccupied many of them for some years. It was only later that many of their thoughts returned to England and the heady days at Thorpe Abbotts.

For others, plans to retain contact with former comrades were almost immediate and Captain Bill Carleton was determined to keep in touch with the '351st Squadron Line.'

He wrote and distributed a Christmas letter on 17 December 1946 and continued this practice down the years. The letters contained all the news he had gleaned during the year about the 351st men and snippets regarding other 100th people. Later, he also corresponded with the Drapers and the Taylor and Hurry families back in Dickleburgh.

Along with other 100th 'notables' Bill Carleton was a driving force in the 100th Bomb Group Association in the U.S.A.

On 18 December 1961 Bill's annual note reported on a letter from me: 'Sam sent along four snapshots of the old aerodrome, including one of the 351st Technical Supply. We are sure that Cummings will be pleased to know this edifice is still standing. Sam is managing a shoe store and is in the Civil Defence in the capacity of a Sector Commander. Another picture he sent was of the Control Tower which is still on its feet – but just barely.'

Bill's December 1963 letter included a copy of a letter to him and his wife Mary from the Taylors. Dated 4 December 1963, it read:

'Just a letter hoping you are all well, and I am pleased to say we are very well. I am also enclosing a note that I had given to me from an officer that was on the base. (Chaplin, Lt. Col. Glenn F. Taska). This has been our Golden Wedding year (January 11, 1963). It was a wonderful time for us both with our friends and relatives all meeting at a party. We had only one disappointment and that was my daughter could not be here owing to an accident. I am sorry to say she is not too good yet. She was knocked down by a car and had a very badly broken leg which causes her to walk lame and she still has a lot of pain. Bill is still working a machine mixing material for road mending at Chelmsford. His two children are growing up now, both going to school. Our son, George, is at home with us and has a herd of pigs. He still works for Mr. W. Draper. They are all busy now getting the sugar beet off the fields before the bad weather sets in. It is a sharp frost this morning. I hope we don't get the weather as bad this winter as last year. It was the worst I've ever known.

I expect your family are getting quite grown up now. We have not seen or heard from any of the men we knew from the war time. I hope you will kindly remember us to any that you still include in your yearly letter. I think this is all for this time.

Yours very sincerely, George and Eleanor Taylor and family.'

Other veterans were able to travel to Europe down the years and to visit Thorpe Abbotts in its deteriorated and forlorn state. One newspaper report, dated 2 September 1977, recalled one such visit:

'From the balcony of the control tower General John Bennett surveyed the open expanse of cornfields and recalled the anxious hours he stood in that same spot waiting for 'his boys' to return........The control tower is now a cracked and crumbling shadow of its former self, but for the general the fact that it still stands is remarkable in itself. 'It is here. That is all that matters,' he said with feeling.

'While the Americans recalled their war days at Thorpe Abbotts, William Draper and his sister Alda, were able to tell them of even earlier days. They can recall the aerodrome being laid – the main runway went straight across Mr. Draper's farmland!

'The Drapers joined Saturdays reunion, bringing with them a more tangible memory of the airfield's glory days – a bottle of U.S.A.A.F. imported port, given to them as a gift by grateful American servicemen. 'They didn't like the base water and used to come and get it from us,' said Mr. Draper. His sister remembered that they used to have a pass to get to their home across their own land.'

RESTORATION
Restoration   Mrs. Pearson's Letter
Munster Mayor Official   Artifacts

I joined the group about six months after the start of the restoration of the Control Tower. This came about by my annual return to Thorpe Abbotts to take photographs of various buildings etc. I did this from 1950 and sent these to Bill Carleton who I corresponded with through the fifties to date.

On arrival at the Control Tower there was a clearance of shrubbery and grass around the building. After making enquiries I found out that a few local people had started to restore the Control Tower. I joined the group and became an active decorator, amongst other things.

Our meetings were held in the top room of the Control Tower, sitting on oil drums and scaffold boards. I could foresee a situation of becoming better organised and eventually I was elected as secretary and editor of the members' newsletter, the 'Century Bulletin.'

I drafted up the Rules and regulations, a Constitution and eventually obtained Charity Registration for the Museum.

The Tower in 1977. (100th BGMM)

Sam and son Robert on restoration work. (Sam Hurry)

Some lighter moments were often had with Mike Harvey and his moped fetching a one hundredweight bag of cement from Diss on the back rack. In those days it was a struggle to obtain materials. I seemed to be continually scrounging materials from firms; paint, sand, gravel, lawnmowers; you name it, we went for it.

Our eating arrangements were basic: sandwiches in the cold and toilet facilities that were just two sheets of ply nailed together.

Most weekends were spent at the Tower; I think all told I painted it outside twice, inside three times, while others were doing other work. Another lighter moment was during pitching of the roof, when Ron Batley ended up covered in tar and pitch.

The volunteers, including Mike Harvey, Ron Batley, Ken Everett, Richard Gibson, Paul Meen and myself, worked in all weathers, including when snow falls blanketed the airfield. John Goldsmith was another early joiner to the group. Both Ken and John had been schoolboys during the war years and had many memories of the active airfield.

I must say, it was difficult to try to keep to rules and follow procedures with all of us being volunteers.

Mike Harvey, whose dream it was to restore the Tower, was not always looking at being organised but he did support me in my efforts for the Museum.

Mrs. Pearson, widow of John D. Pearson, lived in New York and wrote to me on June 28th 1979:

Dear Friends

Thank you very much for your kind note about John, I appreciate these words more than you know. I have a cat called Buffie, he just celebrated his eighth year of life – it's good to have him since John is gone. This character understands every word I say – it's a mutual admiration society. John told me all about you and how much help you gave to him during the war. Yes, I would like a picture of John – a copy of the one John is in. You are very kind to think of me.

Maybe you could write a book called 'Living with the 8th Air Force' or 'My childhood memories with the 8th Air Force during World War II.'

Take care, all my best to all of you,

Dora Pearson (Widow of John D. Pearson).

On 12 August 1980 Bill Carleton wrote to me: 'Your news on the progress with the Control Tower at Thorpe Abbotts is welcome news. Some of these days, Mary and I hope to visit the museum. After all, we can't let General Bennett get ahead of us. As you know, the Tower was located within the '351st Line.' Consequently, I was in and around it several times a day as we went about our chores to 'Keep 'Em Flying.'

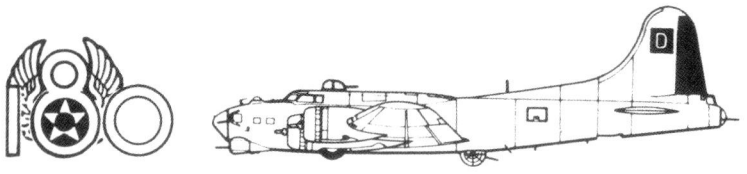

100th BOMB GROUP MEMORIAL MUSEUM.   REGISTERED CHARITY No. 285169
THORPE ABBOTTS, NORFOLK.

request the pleasure of

To the OFFICIAL OPENING of the

100th Bomb Group Memorial Museum

on JUNE 4th 1983 at 11 am

R.S.V.P. to the Secretary, April 30th.

The Museum Opening Invitation 1983. (100th BGMM)

The 1986 Reunion, B-17 'Sally-B' overhead. (Malcolm Finnis)

Bill's Christmas 1980 letter referred to me having sent pictures and film of the Tower restoration and my planned visit to the U.S. He continued: 'Needless to say, all of us are looking forward to welcoming Sam, the little laundry boy, who used to sit wide eyed, as he listened to the tales of the war and life in the States.'

The Mayor's Officer from Munster, Hubert Kosters, attended the dedication of the Museum on 21 May 1981. During the war Herr Kosters was the same age as myself and he came with his daughter Sigrid for the official opening the Museum. He lived through the bombing of Munster, while I saw the take-off and return of the planes from Thorpe Abbotts that same Sunday.

He came and represented the city of Munster at our event. I got on very well with him and his daughter as I could speak German, although not fluently, and was able to communicate with them. His explanation of the raid was an interesting tie up with me of the same age and of the 100th's veterans at the opening of the Museum. I was invited to Munster but I never went. It was a privilege to meet them albeit they were from a country that we were at war with. From that visit developed the book by Ian Hawkins about the Munster mission, *'Munster: The Way It Was.'*

One time, during the 1980s, when artefacts were being collected for the museum, Mike Harvey said to me: 'What do you think is in that black bin bag, Sam?' I did not open the bag but could smell the mothball aroma and said: 'It's a parachute.' He asked me how I knew that and I said it was because of the smell. The parachute was from a B-24 Liberator named *'Bird Dog'* that crashed on Acle marshes, it was put in the black bag from its case after being dug up.

1986 Reunion Video cover, Sam bottom left talking to reporter. (100th BGMM)

American journalists visit the Museum, 1991. (Mercury)

American journalist visit 1991, Sam points to his picture. (Mercury)

Sam and Mike Harvey 1993. (Norfolk and Suffolk Express)

REUNIONS
Reunions   Honorary Member   The Generals

Although many unofficial, and largely unrecorded, visits took place at Thorpe Abbotts in the years after the war, formal and organised reunions on the airfield commenced with the restoration of the Control Tower and the official opening on 4 June 1983. As mentioned, the Tower was dedicated in May 1981, but only some of the veterans were able to be present. Although the museum was 'open' from that time an official opening was timed for the 1983 reunion on the airfield.

1992 Reunion. (Malcolm Finnis)

Once established, these generally took place in the alternate years to the U.S. reunions. These continued up to 2000 but with the veterans becoming older and fewer, these have now been discontinued. However, some veterans still come over from the U.S.A. to visit Thorpe Abbotts although increasingly the tourists are family members and descendants

The first stateside reunion of the 100th Bomb Group Association (U.S.A.) was held at Andrews Field, Washington D.C. in 1969 and this was followed by a second in Milwaukee in 1973. Subsequent reunions were

Sam at the 2000 Reunion.
(Malcolm Finnis)

held in the U.S.A. every two or three years and continue to the present time.

Jane and I were made honorary members of the U.S. 100th Bomb Group Association, way back in 1979.

I have visited the U.S.A. for the reunions with my colleagues and have been most warmly welcomed. I met up with Frank Valesh's sister a few years ago. While the British Reunions have been covered by the Norfolk press, the *'Eastern Daily Press,'* the *'Diss Express'* and the *'Wymondham and Attleborough Mercury,'* in America coverage has been included in *'The Houston Post,' 'Grand Rapids Press,'* the *'Philadelphia Inquirer'* and many others.

My wife, Jane and I attended five reunions in the U.S.A. We had two sons to raise so money was not flowing for us to attend others.

The first was held at Myrtle Beach in South Carolina. We were overwhelmed by the hospitality of the Americans. It was my first chance to meet up with many of the 100th veterans that I knew during the war. It was an exceptional reunion, one which we enjoyed very much, indeed with a Wendy's beef sandwich, a trip well worth going on. We flew into Miami, Florida and stayed with Snookie Spangler's sister and then went on to Myrtle Beach by road through Georgia. After the reunion we toured Tennessee, Indiana and Chicago. We then made a long train journey to Washington D.C. and stayed there for four days, visiting with Harry Cruver. (In March 1945 Harry

Ken Lemmons at the 2000 Reunion.
(Malcolm Finnis)

Bob and Snookie Spangler with Sam. (Sam Hurry)

Sam receiving his 'Luckye Bastardes' certificate
l-r Irv Waterbury, Sam, 'Storm' Rhode. front Gen. O'Malley. (Sam Hurry)

Sam's 'Luckye Bastardes' Certificate. (Sam Hurry)

led the formations on the final offensive aerial sweep by the 100th on Berlin).

The second reunion we went to was at Dayton, Ohio. We flew into Philadelphia and stayed at the Martins' (351st Squadron aircrew), in South Jersey. Then we motored to Dayton through some of the best countryside I have ever seen. Whilst at Millville, New Jersey, there was a welcome by the Fire Service, the Police, the local Legion, and other people, organised by Lewis and Doris Martin. Dayton was indeed a large reunion where again we saw and met many of the veterans that I knew from their days of wartime service.

During the war the 8th Air Force Luckye Bastardes Club was founded for those aircrew who carried out the required number of missions, and returned safely, to complete a tour of duty. Each member was given a certificate outlining the experience in laboured old English script. At the Dayton Reunion I was awarded an honorary membership in the Luckye Bastardes Club and ceremonially awarded my certificate.

After the reunion we headed to Cleveland and dined in the 100th Restaurant owned by Dave Tallichet (ex-aircrew). We then travelled on to Niagra, and spent two days there being shown around by a veteran who lived nearby. It was an eye-opener; I was aghast at the sights. We returned to Millville following the Susquana River down through Pennsylvania, and stopping off in Amish country. Whilst in South Jersey we visited Atlantic City and went to the casinos. We then flew home from Philadelphia after another excellent trip.

Long Beach, California was the venue for our third reunion. We flew to Bozeman, Montana to stay a few days with the Drysdales (ex-pilot), and what a stay. It was way beyond what I had expected. It took two days to get used to the altitude in Montana. We then made our way south to Long Beach, allowing a week to tour on the way. This was the largest reunion ever with around thirteen hundred people attending.

Yellowstone, Bryce Canyon, Grand Canyon and many more places were monumental visits that were just out of this world. We visited Death Valley, refreshed ourselves at Kingsman and spent three days in Las Vegas. We visited the Hoover Dam and the Painted Desert. We stayed in Flagstaff, Arizona and had a very good time. It was nice to meet up with old friends and whilst in Long Beach we visited the *'Queen Mary'* and the *'Spruce Goose.'* We had a tour of Los Angeles and flew home from there.

Our fourth reunion was at Fort Worth, Texas. As usual, we enjoyed meeting with old friends. It was a good reunion, but some faces were missing. After the reunion we went to Richards, Texas to stay with relatives, and later visited Galveston and Houston; we had a a grand time. On this occasion we flew in to Fort Worth and left from Houston.

The fifth reunion was held at Cincinnati, Ohio in 1999. I did not feel this was a good reunion for the Brits, so I will leave this here. We came home after four days.

Overall, Jane and I managed to visit, or stay in 28 states: Arizona, California, Colorado, Connecticut, Delaware, Florida, Georgia, Idaho, Illinois, Indiana, Kentucky, Maryland, Michigan, Minnesota, Montana, Nevada, New Jersey, New York, North Carolina, Ohio, Pennsylvania, South Carolina, Tennessee, Texas, Utah, Virginia, West Virginia and the District of Columbia.

The U.S. service people at R.A.F. Mildenhall in Suffolk always treated me with great respect and on visits and at air shows I was asked to wear a V.I.P. badge which opened many doors!

Cincinnati Reunion 1999.
l-r Sam, Jane, Malcolm Finnis, front F. McDermot, Harry Cruver. (Malcolm Finnis)

In May 1995 the Commanding Officer of the 100th Air Refuelling Wing invited me to take part in R.A.F. Mildenhall's Honorary Commander Program. As Honorary Commander of the 95th Reconnaissance Squadron I would have been invited to a variety of functions on the base throughout the year, including change of command ceremonies. I had to decline with thanks as, at the time, my health was not as it should have been.

I also sat on the Anglo-American committee which consisted of Americans and British representatives with the main aim of fostering U.S.-Anglo relations. Whenever I went to Mildenhall I dined in the Officers' Club and over the years spoke with many commanders of the 100th Air Refuelling Wing and of the 3rd Air Force and developed the friendships that have continued to this day.

Over the years I have made contact with many U.S.A.F. stations and cemeteries and answered questions and queries for people back in the U.S. I have written to very high ranking people, both military and civil. I have corresponded, and made friends with, some of the household names of the 100th aircrew that I would have only seen glimpses of as a boy.

Major General James G. Andrus, USAF
Commander, United States Third Air Force
and
Colonel James W. Morehouse, USAF
Commander, 100th Air Refueling Wing
request the pleasure of the company of
Mr. & Mrs. Sam Hurry
at Air Fete '95
commemorating the fiftieth anniversary of the
end of the Second World War
on Sunday, the twenty-eighth of May, 1995
Reception at eleven o'clock, followed by buffet luncheon at twelve o'clock
in the Passenger Terminal, RAF Mildenhall

RSVP by 12 May 1995
Secretary, 100 ARW/CC, RAF Mildenhall, Suffolk IP28 8NF   Service Dress or Lounge Suit

Sam's Mildenhall Air Fete Invitation 1995. (Sam Hurry)

The contacts made included several generals:

General Curtis E. LeMay,
Commanding Officer 3rd Air Division (that included the 100th B.G.). In 1961 he became Chief of Staff of the United States Air Force.

General LeMay invited Jane and I to lunch while we were at the Long Beach Reunion. A very interesting man, he was very alert and very much up to date.

Major General Thomas S. Jeffrey Jr.,
100th Bomb Group Commanding Officer 9.5.44 – 1.2.45

We met General Jeffrey at the same meeting as General LeMay. Both generals were talking about the Middle East, LeMay left Jeffrey in no doubt how he would deal with the Middle East problem, and went on to pull rank on Jeffrey and down-sized him in front of all others present. It was done to show who was the senior rank. LeMay's wife said: 'Nobody won when Curtis LeMay was on his feet;' she had him cut and dried to a 'T'.

Major General John Bennett,
Acting Commanding Officer 100th B.G. twice in early 1944

I often spoke to John Bennett, by phone, letter or in person. He was a great thinking man and he did ask me for advice on different things. He was a gentleman.

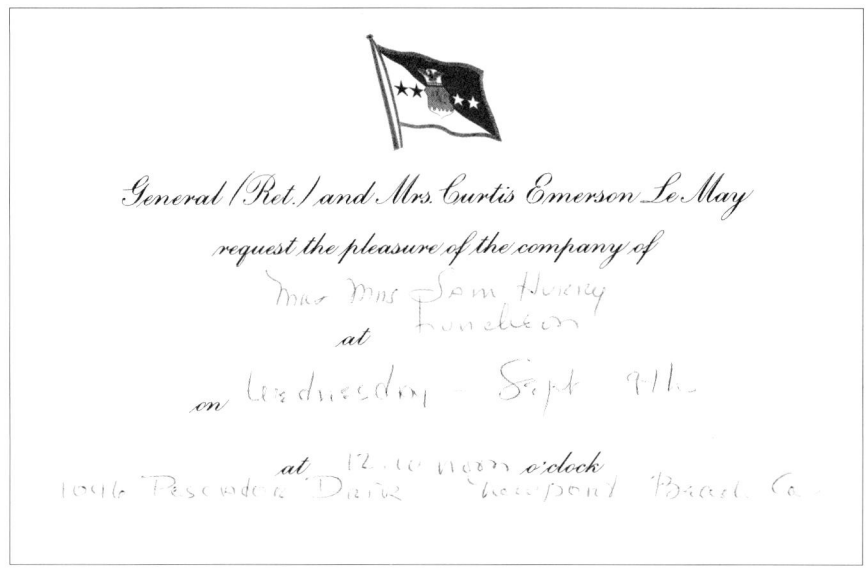

Invitation from General Le May. (Sam Hurry)

General James Doolittle,
Commanding Officer 8th U.S.A.A.F.
I was invited to meet General Doolittle at Cambridge who kindly signed a 100th photograph for me, about 1980, whilst he was having breakfast with the Pennowes'. Mrs. Pennowe was a representative of the 8th Air Force Historical Society.

Lieutenant General H. Schuler.
I first spoke to General Schuler whilst he was helping to establish the 8th Air Force Museum in Georgia and we discussed possible exhibits and plans for the museum. Without General Schuler's involvement I doubt if the museum would have gone ahead. He flew out to Thorpe Abbotts, via Mildenhall, from Germany and I met him to discuss the 8th Museum plans.

Many more high ranking officers spoke with me and helped us along the road to restoration.

Meeting these generals played an important part in my life. I do recall that on one occasion I needed to speak to a high ranking air force man about transportation. He said he could make the time by me going gliding with him at R.A.F. Marham. Once in the air he and I had a good conversation, and some scary flying.

Whenever the Boeing B-52s came to Marham I was invited to go and meet the crews and to look over the airplanes.

UP TO THE PRESENT

On New Years Day 1991, Bill Carleton wrote: 'This will mark my 45th Christmas letter to the 351st Line, and I think it is time for me to hang up my pen.'

Very little now exists of the once vibrant airbase although part of the northern perimeter remains, along with Dispersal 5, the Control Tower and the Ambulance Shed. The small Pyrotechnic Store has been incorporated into the Museum's Varian Centre, again as a store. Further along Common Road, Grove Wood looks just the same as it did during the 100th's presence with the Battle Headquarters still guarding the empty airfield.

The demolition of Grove Cottage was never completely cleared away and even today some rubble, well covered by grass, remains on the small site.

Today the Museum is an Accredited Museum and a Registered Charity. It is well known and respected in Great Britain, Europe and the U.S.A. with several thousand visitors each year. The Museum attracts local, national and foreign visitors as individuals, groups and special interest clubs.

Mike Harvey sadly died in May 1995 but Ron, Ken, Richard, John and myself continue as trustees and Paul as a member. Jean Harvey, Norma Gibson and Carol Batley have been closely involved in the success of the Museum from the beginning and carry on their valued commitment today.

The Red Cross Hut in 1993. (Malcolm Finnis)

Night flight in 100th Air Refuelling Wing KC-135R 1998 (Malcolm Finnis)

The Tower in 2004, Grove Wood in background. (Malcolm Finnis)

Sam's birthplace at left, in 2008.

'The Crown' Dickleburgh in 2008.

The old 'King's Head' Dickleburgh 2008, now a private house.

The old Taylor house in 2008.

The old Hurry house in Common Road 2008.

Malcolm Finnis

APPENDIX

One of the original B-17 Fortresses in the early part of the 100th's campaign was *'Piccadilly Lily'* of the 351st Squadron that had Dispersal 8 next to the Control Tower. *'Piccadilly Lily'* went on the famous Schweinfurt/Regensburg raid of 17 August 1943, the 100th's bombers flying to Regensburg and then on as a shuttle mission to North Africa.

One of the officers on that Dakota flight to Britain in February 1942, Beirne Lay Jnr., went on the Regensburg mission as an observer for Eighth Air Force Headquarters, flying as the co-pilot of *'Piccadilly Lily.'* Beirne Lay later wrote the epic story of the bitter air battle over Holland and Germany on that mission, which he described as 'beyond fiction.'

In early October 1943 the 100th operated three days running and the traumatic events of these missions, in which two of the four squadron commanders were lost, wrote a searing chapter in the history of 'The Bloody Hundredth.'

On the 8th October the 100th went to Bremen. Of the 21 aircraft despatched 7 were shot down and 9 returned with damage, some serious. One B-17 came back 400 miles to Thorpe Abbotts on one engine. One of the aircraft lost was *'Piccadilly Lily'* with six of her gallant crew killed. The next day the target was Marienburg although there were no losses. On the 10th October the 100th went to Munster, with some crews operating three days running, too tired to care where they went. The result was as recorded in my tale.

Colonel Beirne Lay Jnr. went on to complete a tour of missions with the 8th Air Force. He later co-wrote the script for the famous film *'Twelve O'clock High'*, in which *'Piccadilly Lily'* featured as did another of the 100ths B-17s, *'The Reluctant Dragon.'*

The Flight Chief, with responsibility for Dispersals 8 through to 11, was Master Sergeant Kenneth A. Lemmons and he vividly recalled his days looking after the B-17s when he returned to Thorpe Abbotts for the 2000 Reunion there.

BOOK LIST
Some books about the 100th Bomb Group

Letters From England J. M. Bennett   John M. Bennett 1945 and subsequent
The Bloody Hundredth Edited by Horace L. Varian 100th B.G. Association 1979
Munster: The Way It Was Ian Hawkins   Hawkins 1984
Century Bombers Richard Le Strange 100th Bomb Group Memorial Museum 1989
With Crew 13 Earl Benham   Earl Benham   1990
A Wing And A Prayer Harry H. Crosby   Robson   1993
A Year In The Life Of A Cowboy Owen D. Roane Ulon   1995, 2003
The Forgotten Man – The Kenneth A. Lemmons Story Cindy Goodman & Jan Ridling
On Target Charles E. (Chuck) Harris   Charles E. Harris 2000
Plane Names And Bloody Noses Volume 2 Ray Bowden   Design Oracle 2000
Return Ticket Carl R. Carlson The Watercress Press   2001
Luck Of The Draw Frank D. Murphy FNP 2001
Memories And Stories Of The 100th Bomb Group Robert Tienken Tienken 2004.

Some books that include the 100th Bomb Group

The Mighty Eighth Roger A. Freeman   Macdonald 1970 and subsequent
Big Week Glenn Infield   Nel   1974
Airfields Of The Eighth - Then And Now   After The Battle   1978 and subsequent
Decision Over Schweinfurt Thomas M. Coffey Magnum 1980
The Mighty Eighth War Diary Roger A. Freeman Jane's 1981
One Last Look Philip Kaplan and Rex Alan Smith Abbeville 1983
Castles In The Air Martin Bowman Patrick Stevens 1984
The Mighty Eighth In Colour Roger A. Freeman Arms & Armour 1991
Memorials To The Mighty Eighth Dennis F. Lain   Serendipity 2004

Naval Group Billy Taylor front row extreme right (Peggy Taylor)

Billy Taylor
(Peggy Taylor)

Ernest Hurry in Norwich Market
(Sam Hurry)

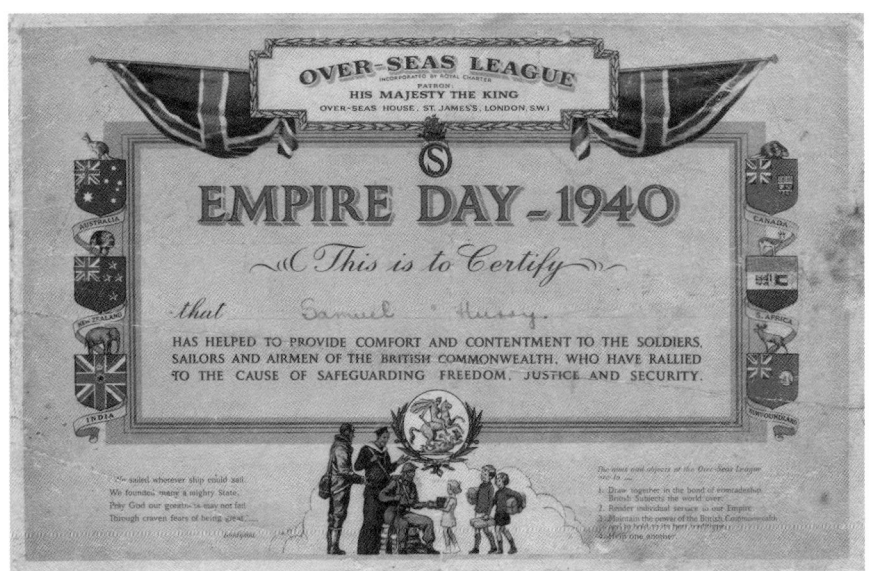

Sam's Empire Day Certificate (Sam Hurry)

Sam and Jane's Sons,
Simon and Robert circa 1985
(Sam Hurry)

Jane and Sam at Cincinnati 1999
(Sam Hurry)